Conte

AREA MAP SHOWING THE LOCATION OF THE WALKS

WATERSIDE WALKS
In Oxfordshire

David Dunford

COUNTRYSIDE BOOKS
NEWBURY, BERKSHIRE

First published 2000
© David Dunford 2000

All rights reserved. No reproduction
permitted without the prior permission
of the publisher:

COUNTRYSIDE BOOKS
3 Catherine Road
Newbury, Berkshire

To view our complete range of books,
please visit us at
www.countrysidebooks.co.uk

ISBN 1 85306 630 3

For Michelle

Designed by Graham Whiteman
Maps by the author
Photographs by the author and Dawn Gordon

Produced through MRM Associates Ltd., Reading
Printed by Woolnough Bookbinding Ltd., Irthlingborough

Walk

PUBLISHER'S NOTE

We hope that you obtain considerable enjoyment from this book; great care has been taken in its preparation. However, changes of landlord and actual closures are sadly not uncommon. Likewise, although at the time of publication all routes followed public rights of way or permitted paths, diversion orders can be made and permissions withdrawn.

We cannot, of course, be held responsible for such diversion orders and any inaccuracies in the text which result from these or any other changes to the routes nor any damage which might result from walkers trespassing on private property. We are anxious though that all details covering the walks and the pubs are kept up to date and would therefore welcome information from readers which would be relevant to future editions.

INTRODUCTION

Walking beside water is always interesting and in Oxfordshire there are many opportunities – not least because of the presence of the River Thames and its tributaries. When it enters the county near Lechlade, the Thames is near to the limit of navigation; there is only one lock upstream of the county boundary. By the time, some 26 locks later, that it leaves the county near Henley it has grown into a mature river. While passing through Oxfordshire, the Thames is swollen by the waters of the Cole, the Windrush, the Evenlode (which in turn is fed by the Glyme and the Dorn), the Cherwell, the Ock, the Ginge Brook and the Thame. The walks in this book include sections of most of these rivers, as well as the Thames itself, the Oxford Canal, and a number of lesser streams and watercourses. I have tried to include walks from all areas of this rich and varied county, but obviously some of the drier chalk country is not conducive to waterside walking. Geography also dictates the slight preponderance of walks in the north-western quarter of Oxfordshire, where many of the county's rivers flow.

For each walk I include a brief taste of the route, then a slightly fuller description of some of its features, including details of at least one pleasant pub (often a waterside one). A logistical section then explains how to get to the start, where to park, how long the walk is and which Ordnance Survey maps to take with you. I hope and believe that you should be able to find your way around the routes using the descriptions and sketch maps provided. However, a more general map, particularly one from the excellent new Explorer series, will always add to your appreciation of a walk and will prove useful if, as I hope, you choose to adapt or extend the routes in this book.

All the walks are circular, start and end at the recommended pub, and generally avoid obscure or hard-to-follow paths. I have also tried to minimise road walking, busy roads and sections that need to be walked twice. All routes are on public rights of way or permitted paths, and vary from $3^1/_4$ to $6^3/_4$ miles in length (though the longest can be shortened very easily), which should be a viable half-day proposition for any walker of average fitness. After a full route description, the account of each walk ends with notes of a nearby attraction, plus a telephone number where appropriate (and sometimes a web address) for more information, so that you can plan a full day out if you wish.

A word of warning should be given to winter walkers: the Thames and its larger tributaries are prone to flooding – indeed, this has shaped the agriculture of the Thames valley and largely accounts for the undeveloped landscape along the riverbank. Many of the routes described on these pages may prove impassable after heavy rain (although probable exceptions suitable for damp periods include Walks 3, 4, 5, 18 and 20). At many other times of year, it is an inevitable feature of waterside walks that you will encounter mud and sometimes lush growth along the way. I would recommend boots and long trousers except in the very best of weather.

I would like to thank the following friends and colleagues who helped me make this book as useful as possible by checking the route descriptions and offering many valuable suggestions: Namira and Ian; Duncan, Rachel and Sarah; Victoria Fretwell, Daniel Goodwin, Kate Samways and Stephen Scowcroft; Dawn Gordon; Kerry Hall; Jane Hunt; Lin, Rob and Ben Merrick; Chris Prosser and Helen Jamieson; Jon Uren and family; Steve Roby and family; Matt Scantlebury; Phil and Helen Spearman; André and Cindy Tansley; Helen and Derek Wright.

Please respect the rights of other users of the countryside and its rivers – landlords, farmers and landowners, anglers, boaters and lock-keepers – when you visit, and try to leave no mark of your passing on the land. I sincerely hope that you will discover some new favourites, or rediscover some old ones, while following the walks described between the covers of this book.

David Dunford

WALK 1

THE CHERWELL AND THE OXFORD CANAL AT CROPREDY

The name of Cropredy will be familiar to folk music buffs: the band Fairport Convention has held an annual folk festival here for many years. However, when the festival is not in town it's a quiet and pretty ironstone village on a popular stretch of the Oxford Canal, with the River Cherwell flowing close by. Neighbouring Wardington and Williamscot are similarly attractive villages, set in rolling north Oxfordshire countryside.

The Oxford Canal

The Battle of Cropredy Bridge took place during the Civil War on 29th June 1644, in fields east of the river. A Parliamentary army of 9,500 clashed with a slightly smaller Royalist force under King Charles I. The King subsequently spent a couple of nights in nearby Williamscot, though he avoided the manor due to an outbreak of smallpox. The battle was considered a notable success for the Royalist side, but was

8

overshadowed by their devastating defeat at Marston Moor just three days later. Echoes of the battle abound: the modern bridge over the Cherwell includes a commemoration stone and the church register records the burial of soldiers.

It seems surprising that the name of a humble Cropredy shepherd should still be known to this day, even more that the association should be with the pharmaceutical industry. One Thomas Beecham once tended the flocks at Cropredy Lawn, a farm still existing in the village. The tablet on which his wife rolled the original 'Beecham's pills' survived within recent memory.

The Oxford Canal runs from the Thames at Oxford to the Grand Union Canal at Napton in Warwickshire. It was designed by James Brindley in the 1780s to transport freight from the industrial Midlands to the Thames and is now a popular route for pleasure craft (and walkers, who can follow the entire length along the towpath).

The Red Lion at Cropredy is a lovely thatched ironstone building in a beautiful setting by the church. Within it is cosy, with central heating *and* a log fire ensuring a warm welcome in winter. The 15th-century building, which has been an inn since the mid-18th century, is said to be haunted. The pub is open all day in summer (and normal opening hours in winter). Four real ales are on offer plus 'typically English' food. You are advised to book if you are part of a large group or are planning to eat during summer weekends. Telephone: 01295 750224.

- **HOW TO GET THERE:** Cropredy can be reached from the A361 Banbury–Daventry road via Williamscot, or from the A423 Banbury–Southam road via Great Bourton. Either way, leave the principal road through the village along a lane north by the canal bridge and follow it to Red Lion Street.
- **PARKING:** There is limited parking at the Red Lion; please ask the bar staff before leaving your car while you walk, or park in the nearby roads.
- **LENGTH OF THE WALK:** $5^3/_4$ miles. Maps: OS Landranger 151 Stratford-upon-Avon, Warwick and Banbury; OS Pathfinder 1022 Banbury (North) (GR 469467).

THE WALK

1. Walk down Red Lion Street to the canal and cross the bridge (signposted to Prescote). Walk left along the metalled track with the canal on your left and the River Cherwell to your right. Swing right, following the Cherwell, as you approach Prescote Manor, once home

9

to a colourful 17th-century pamphleteer, Walter Gostelow. This is a significant point in the northward journey of the Oxford Canal, where it leaves the Cherwell valley for the first and last time. Keep along the track past the manor and on towards Prescote Manor Farm (the actual right-of-way runs parallel through the field on the left). Just before you reach the farm, turn right through a small conifer wood and cross the River Cherwell.

2. Keep along the field edge as it climbs the valley side. At the top of the hill you enter a field with impressive ridge and furrow; keep left until you reach the main road at a gate. There is a glimpse of the lake of Wardington House as you walk uphill to the right. When you reach a road junction by the Hare and Hounds pub, turn left (signposted to Edgcote). When the road swings right, cross a stile on the right and walk along a path that follows a small stream. Keep along the stream as it flows through more fields of ridge and furrow on the left with the village of Wardington above you to the right. Eventually after a pleasant ½ mile or so the stream leads you to Upper Wardington. Walk around the green to the left then double-back right at the top of the green when you meet the 'main' road and walk through the rest of the village. Keep left past Wardington Manor, passing Barn Farm Plants, then keep right at a farm building with a sign reading 'Top Dawkins' where the road to Chacombe leads off to the left.

3. When you reach the A361, turn left for a short distance then take a path on the right. This cuts the corner to bring you out onto the road at the beginning of Williamscot village. Turn right, then left into another lane, passing a telephone box. When the road swings left follow a footpath straight on (through a farm). This leads above an obvious spring then swings right through yet more ridge and furrow (with views to Williamscot House on the right) to a gate close to the Cherwell. Beyond the gate the path leads parallel to the river then crosses it via a footbridge near the remains of Slat Mill. The Parliamentarian forces forded the Cherwell near here in 1644.

4. Our route climbs slightly to the canal, joins the towpath to the left of the bridge and follows it right (northwards). Keep along the canal for just over a mile, passing the remains of an early 19th-century mill at Bourton House halfway along, until you reach the bridge at Cropredy. The site of the battle is close to the Cherwell bridge (to your right) but

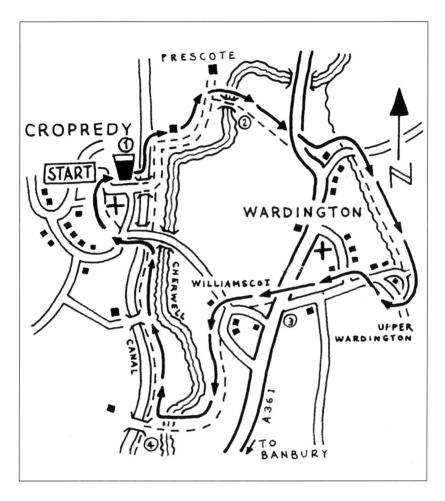

our route crosses the canal to the left and then turns immediately right. Shortly afterwards, a walled path on the left leads between gardens to the churchyard, beyond which is journey's end.

PLACES OF INTEREST NEARBY

Banbury Museum in the Horsefair overlooks Banbury Cross, in the centre of the town. It is housed in the former boardroom of the Poor Law Guardians and its permanent exhibits, which tell the story of 'Banburyshire', are supplemented by regular temporary exhibitions. Telephone: 01295 259855.

STEEPLE ASTON AND THE HEYFORDS: BY RIVER AND CANAL

For much of its length, the Oxford Canal follows the valley of the River Cherwell (see also Walk 1). This circuit samples both waterways in an attractive part of the valley. Steeple Aston and Upper and Lower Heyford are delightful villages. Fine views of valley and village, a rustic 'folly' on a hillside, an impressive tithe barn and a babbling spring are some of the highlights of this rewarding walk.

The Oxford Canal at Upper Heyford

Steeple Aston is an attractive ironstone village based around parallel lanes either side of a steep-sided valley. As at Steeple Barton (see Walk 3), the name does not imply that the church ever had a spire – 'steeple' was used to refer to an unfortified tower. The church is originally 13th century and contains some fine monuments. The remains of a medieval cross stand in the churchyard. Just outside the village, and seen twice during this walk, is the 'Rousham Eyecatcher', a rustic arched folly of

12

ironstone, which was constructed to add interest to the view from Rousham House (to the south) by the architect and landscape gardener William Kent in 1738.

For many inhabitants of Oxfordshire, the name of Upper Heyford conjures up unlikely images of screaming jets and vociferous protestors. However, the USAF airfield ceased operations in the early 1990s and peace has descended once more on the nearby villages. Upper Heyford church is largely Victorian, but has its original Perpendicular tower. More authentic is the tithe barn of around 1400 that stands beside the church on a high bank overlooking the canal. Lower Heyford is a larger village, with pretty cottages leading down to the swing-bridge over the canal. The Heyfords were named after a ford where hay was carried across the Cherwell; a bridge on the site (not visited on this walk) has part of the original 13th-century structure remaining.

The Red Lion at Steeple Aston has produced what amounts to a manifesto for pubs, available on a printed leaflet. It bemoans the decline of the traditional public house and vows that the Red Lion will be faithful to the ideals of the 'talkers' pub' - no games machines, no music, 'fair fodder', real ale and good company - and it certainly succeeds. The comfortable bar serves local Hook Norton and a rotating guest beer, and bar food is available from 12 noon to 2 pm every day of the week; the dining room, with a full à la carte menu and a choice of 120 wines, is open from 6.30 pm to 9.30 pm on Tuesday to Saturday evenings (booking advised). The cooking is of a high standard and includes seasonal items, such as salads and seafood in summer, and game and other hearty dishes in the winter. There is a pleasant floral terrace (to which children are restricted). Telephone: 01869 340225.

- **HOW TO GET THERE:** Steeple Aston is just off the A4260 Oxford–Banbury road. From the south take the first turning signposted to the village after Hopcroft's Holt. The Red Lion is soon encountered, on the left at the junction with Water Lane.
- **PARKING:** There is limited parking at the pub (please ask if you wish to leave your car while you walk), but you should be able to find a space in South Side.
- **LENGTH OF THE WALK:** 4 miles. Maps: OS Landranger 164 Oxford, Chipping Norton and Bicester; OS Explorer 191 Banbury, Bicester and Chipping Norton (GR 471259).

THE WALK

1. From the terrace of the Red Lion descend the steps and turn left down Water Lane. This drops to the stream and then climbs to reach North Side. Turn right and walk along the village lane, past attractive ironstone buildings, to the church. At the junction, cross over and head slightly right into Cow Lane. Just by the last house, follow the footpath on the left over a stile (signposted for the Cherwell Valley Walk). At the bottom of the field you briefly rejoin Cow Lane, but turn left immediately through a metal gate to follow a path along the left-hand edge of the field, with the Rousham Eyecatcher prominent to your right. At the end of the field, a gate takes you through a hedge; walk straight down the next field, parallel to the hedge on your right. At the bottom of the field, walk down through a belt of trees and across a footbridge over part of the Cherwell, then swing right towards the railway bridge over the main river. The path passes under a separate arch to the right of the main span.

Walk along the river to a small weir, where you follow the right-hand branch to a footbridge. Cross this, then walk across to the foot of another bridge. There are bridges here over the Cherwell and then the Oxford Canal, but our route turns right along the towpath between river and canal.

2. Shortly you pass Allen's Lock (you can cross the canal via the bridge here if you wish to explore the village). A little further along the towpath you pass beneath Upper Heyford church and the fine tithe barn atop a steep bank. Keep on along the canal for a further mile to the swing-bridge at Lower Heyford (where, again, you may decide to cross the canal and explore the village).

3. Our route passes the gates of the mill house on the right then immediately takes a path on the right, signposted to Steeple Aston and heading away from the canal through a metal gate. This path crosses the two legs of the Cherwell below the mill, and follows a further placid sidestream until you reach a stile into a field. Here leave the stream and walk diagonally to a bridge over the railway in the far left-hand corner of the field.

4. Beyond the railway, follow the left-hand edge of the field. A stile leads into a wooded section. At the end of this stretch, with the Rousham Eyecatcher again prominent to your right, keep along the left-hand side of the next two fields. Just beyond a kissing gate by a field

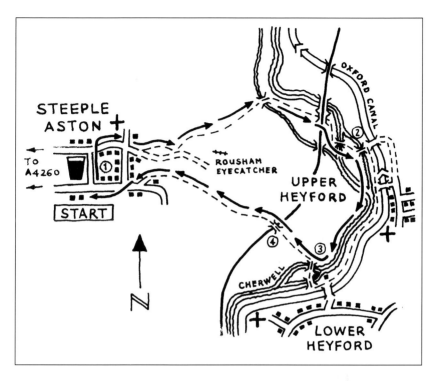

gate, close to the path on your left but hidden among trees and bushes, is Duckworth's Well. At the end of this field, a further kissing gate leads to the end of a concrete track, which crosses the stream at the bottom of the valley then climbs to the appropriately named End Cottage at the bottom of a lane. Follow the lane up to the main village street by the White Lion pub. Turn right, then keep straight on past the old-fashioned post office on the corner, passing a procession of handsome ironstone cottages and farmhouses, until you return to the Red Lion.

PLACES OF INTEREST NEARBY
Rousham Park is 2 miles to the south of Steeple Aston. The house and gardens were built in 1635 by Sir Robert Dormer, and redesigned in the 18th century by William Kent. The gardens at Rousham, with the ponds and cascades of Venus' Vale, and the Temple of the Mill, are largely unchanged and represent the best surviving example of Kent's work. No dogs, or children under 15. For more information, telephone 01869 347110 or visit the excellent Steeple Aston Online Village at http://www.geocities.com/Heartland/Meadows/ 2410/index.html.

15

THE RIVER DORN AT MIDDLE BARTON AND BARTON ABBEY

A delightful stroll around a pretty streamside village and the grounds of a grand country house. The Dorn is one of Oxfordshire's lesser rivers but flows through some beautiful countryside. This fairly level route is generally free of excessive mud and is a good all-year-round walk.

The River Dorn flowing through Middle Barton

Middle Barton was settled by villagers from nearby Steeple Barton after the plague and grew up along the Dorn and the medieval road from Bicester. It is a large and varied village with two fords, a mill and a large number of attractive houses lining its secret lanes and footpaths.

Steeple Barton is now a tiny hamlet surrounding the church above the valley. It was once much larger, as the humps in the nearby fields, and the hollow ways and green lanes that surround it, testify. The church, a mixture of Cotswold stone and reddish ironstone, is strikingly sited and attractive despite heavy Victorian restoration. 'Steeple' was often used to mean simply 'tower', and there is no evidence that the church ever had a spire. By the porch is a medieval stone coffin which was rescued from use as a water trough at a nearby farm.

The 'big house' (not open to the public) is Barton Abbey, which was originally built around 1524 on the site of a cell of Osney Abbey. The present Tudor-style building is largely Victorian but incorporates 16th and 17th century work, and presents a magnificent picture set in sweeping lawns above the lake. Nearby are medieval fishponds.

The Carpenter's Arms in Middle Barton is a welcoming 17th-century thatched pub. The pub serves a wide range of drinks, including four real ales, and an extensive menu includes sandwiches, jacket potatoes and vegetarian options. There is also a specials board, which changes weekly. The cosy public bar has two fireplaces, and the lounge has a collection of chamber pots hanging from the beams. Dog-owners are requested to keep to the public bar or garden. The latter has a large patio, children's play area, Aunt Sally and barbecues in the summer. The pub is open all day at weekends, and food is served seven days a week at lunchtime and in the evenings. Telephone: 01869 340378.

- **HOW TO GET THERE:** Middle Barton is on the B4030 between the Heyfords and Enstone. From the A4260 Oxford–Banbury road at Hopcroft's Holt follow the B4030 west towards Enstone. The Carpenter's Arms is on your left as you enter the village.
- **PARKING:** There are only six parking spaces in front of the pub, so you are requested to find a parking space somewhere along the nearby streets if possible.
- **LENGTH OF THE WALK:** 3¼ miles. Maps: OS Landranger 164 Oxford, Chipping Norton & Bicester; OS Explorer 191 Banbury, Bicester and Chipping Norton (GR 440258).

THE WALK

1. From the front door of the Carpenter's Arms, turn left towards the village centre. Opposite Holliers Crescent turn left into Jacob's Yard, which passes a thatched cottage and then swings right into a narrow lane, past more attractive houses to Mill Lane. Turn left and walk down to the ford at Barton Mill, crossing the Dorn on the attractive stone-arched footbridge. At the triangle, keep left up the hill. When you reach a road, turn left, past the school. Follow this road for about ½ mile until you reach a crossroads by Church Farm. Carry straight on towards the handsome ironstone tower of Steeple Barton church.

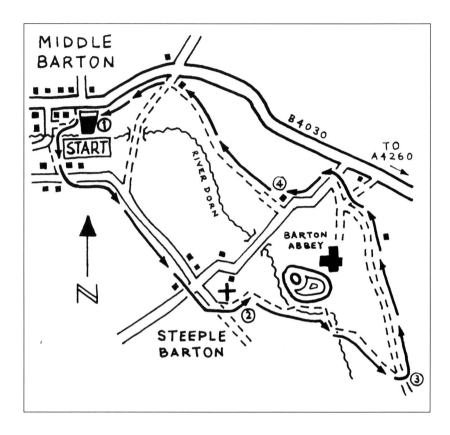

2. Turn left into the churchyard past the porch (noting the stone coffin). In the far right-hand corner you will find a metal gate leading to a yew-shaded path. Follow this left, downhill. Towards the bottom of the hill, the path swings right and leads pleasantly through shrubs and trees. When the path forks, close to the stream, take the left-hand path, which leads via a footbridge over the Dorn to Barton Abbey Lake, beyond which is a spectacular view of the Abbey. Turn right and walk along between lake and river for an all-too-short distance. At the end of this stretch turn right, away from the lake, passing through an arch formed by a whale's jawbone and topped by an appropriately shaped weathervane. Cross the ornamental wooden footbridge and keep left as the other path rejoins. Follow the Dorn past a small ornamental waterfall until you swing left to cross the stream once more by a further ornamental bridge. Beneath a mature horse chestnut tree the path swings right to run through the middle of a clump of slender bamboo.

Beyond this, the path leads to a gate into an area of open parkland. Walk straight up the hill between two horse jumps and follow a line of horse chestnut trees until you reach a gate into a wood at the far end of the field. A short stretch of woodland path leads to a bridleway, at which point you double-back left to a field gate.

3. Follow the track through more parkland, keeping right at the rear of the Abbey near a thatched cricket pavilion. This leads eventually to the entrance road to the Abbey, where you turn right, and cross the impressive avenue to reach the public road. Here turn left and walk downhill for a short distance, following the road down a winding and ivy-clad hollow way.

4. At the first house on the right, with footpath signs in both directions, turn right. This track leads through marshy woodland to a gate into a field. The tall willows on your left conceal the remains of medieval fishponds. Head for the right-hand edge of a copse on the far side of the field. Partway along this copse, a gate on the left leads into the wood. The path leads downhill, slightly overgrown, to a further gate and a footbridge. Beyond this is a brief stretch along the Dorn once more. By the second of two free-standing oak trees, head slightly away from the river, aiming for the left-hand end of a brick cottage at the far end of the field. Beyond a wooden gate by this cottage you reach the B4030. Turn left, past the end of Rayford Lane and walk the short distance back to Middle Barton, crossing the marshy valley of Cockley Brook partway along.

PLACES OF INTEREST NEARBY
Broughton Castle on the B4035 south-west of Banbury can be reached by a delightful drive through the villages of Duns Tew, Hempton, Barford St Michael and Bloxham. The house has featured in many films, most notably *Shakespeare in Love*, *The Madness of King George* and *Three Men and a Little Lady*. The magnificent moated Tudor mansion and its gardens are open to the public on certain days in summer; for more information or to make a booking check the website at http://www.broughtoncastle.demon.co.uk or ring 01295 276070.

THE UPPER GLYME FROM CHURCH ENSTONE

This charming stroll explores the hamlets of the upper Glyme. The infant river is much diverted and dammed to provide a head of water for watermills at Cleveley and Radford, both of which are visited en route. The walk is mostly through attractive pastureland, with one or two areas of semi-natural grassland and woodland for added interest. A few spots may be overgrown or damp underfoot, and there are numerous stiles, but no strenuous climbs.

The river near Radfordbridge

The village of Enstone is named after a prehistoric burial chamber: the Hoar Stone (actually a group of stones of which three remain standing). The village is historically associated with the 'Enstone waterworks'. Thomas Bushell, Master of the King's Mint at Oxford, was clearing a spring on his land when he discovered a remarkable stone, which he named the 'Rock of Enstone'. He proceeded to surround it with a series of artificial fountains, wells and grottoes. The spectacle was described as 'one of the most remarkable hydrostatic displays existing in the kingdom' and 'one of the wonders of Oxfordshire'. King Charles I visited in August 1636, and was so impressed he ordered that the folly be named after his queen. 'Queen Henrietta's Waterworks' fell into disrepair but were restored to even greater glory in the 1770s. However, by the early part of the next century such *jets d'eau* had become unfashionable and little or nothing remains to be seen today.

Enstone, which lay between three important highways, was a favoured stopping-off point in the days of stagecoaches. Its importance can be gauged by the fact that the inhabitants of nearby Charlbury were wont to address their letters 'near Enstone' to ensure safer and quicker delivery, and at one time there were no fewer than nine coaching inns in the village. However, road improvements, the coming of the railways, and the decline in popularity of the waterworks led to the closure of many of these inns.

Cleveley had two or three working mills, of which several remnants can be seen. There is a 'lasher', or waterfall, (a rare survival in Oxfordshire) and a pond that provided a head of water for the waterwheel. Radford too has its mill, again with a lasher.

The Crown Inn at Church Enstone is an ivy-hung, 17th-century pub that manages the delicate act of balancing professional service and quality food with authentic local colour and friendliness. The menu is a cut above normal pub fare: typical choices might be red snapper fillet with salsa and lime butter sauce, or leek and mustard pie. The pub is open normal hours from Monday to Saturday and, conveniently for the weekend walker, all day on Sunday. A selection of real ales and wines by the glass are available. Telephone: 01608 677262.

- **HOW TO GET THERE:** Church Enstone is reached from the A44 between Chipping Norton and Woodstock; travelling from the Woodstock direction, turn right onto the B4022 at the outskirts of Enstone village, then turn left at a crossroads (B4030). The Crown Inn is visible in a side street to the right.

- **PARKING:** There is a small car park at the Crown Inn for patrons only, and limited street parking nearby.

- **LENGTH OF THE WALK:** 5½ miles (full route); 4 miles if you omit the loop from Radfordbridge to Radford Mill and back. Maps: OS Landranger 164 Oxford, Chipping Norton and Bicester; OS Explorer 191 Banbury, Bicester and Chipping Norton (GR 378251).

21

THE WALK

1. From the Crown Inn, walk towards the church. Follow the road round to the right, returning to the main road. Turn left, and shortly right into a road marked 'Unsuitable for heavy goods vehicles' (the irony of this warning will shortly become apparent!). This lane was formerly known as Clingclang Lane because of a noisy gate that once stood here. Follow the narrow lane downhill for approximately 300 yards to the B4022. Cross the road and follow the bridleway opposite (signposted 'Cleveley ¾') alongside the entrance to Drystone Hill House. Once beyond the house, the path begins to descend towards a side valley of the Glyme. At the bottom of the side valley the path swings right and crosses the sidestream by a footbridge. The path enters a shaded track leading to Cleveley. You emerge into a drive, which swings to the right, with a large pond on the left. Cross the Glyme to reach a village lane. A house overlooking the pond has an old arch and twin-light window, which were reused from a 13th or 14th-century ecclesiastical building. Turn left and the lane descends into a shady bridleway alongside the stream. When you reach a wooden footbridge, do not cross – the path immediately bends right, away from the Glyme, uphill to the road. Turn left and then left again at a fork in the road (signposted to Radford).

2. Immediately after the entrance to Cleveley Mill take a footpath on the right, which leads up a steep wooded bank and then crosses a field. At the far side of the field, the path enters a scrubby area and descends in similar vein through intermittent scrub and grassland. After one or two mercifully short overgrown stretches, you regain the Glyme. Keep left through a wooded stretch with the stream on your right. At the end of the wood you cross a stile into a field and keep in the same general direction, negotiating a gate partway along. Beyond this is a delightful stretch where the path follows the meandering stream through a meadow as you approach the road (which lies beyond a gate).

3. At this point, you can shorten your walk by 1½ miles by turning right and resuming from point 4. To continue the main route, turn left and walk uphill through the hamlet of Radfordbridge to a crossroads by some farm buildings, then turn right towards Radford. A short diversion is possible past the no through road sign to view Radford village. Otherwise, turn right down a lane marked 'Unsuitable for motor vehicles' by Radford Farm. Just before the entrance to Radford Mill,

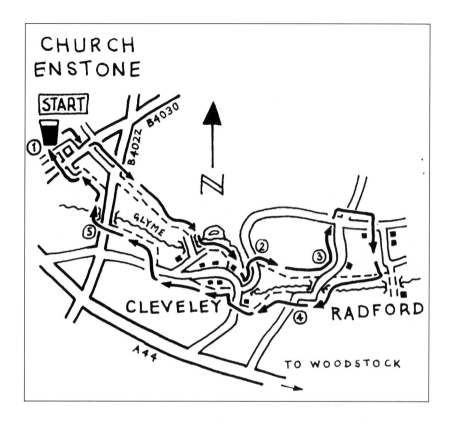

turn right into a field, with the mill leat to the left. After a while the field narrows to pass a pond, then our route leads below the cottages of Radfordbridge once more to regain the road via a stile by the bridge.

4. Cross the bridge and follow the road. When it curves away to the left keep to the Glyme along a footpath that follows a line of pollarded willow trees. Continue with the stream on your right; as the field narrows, go through a gate. As you approach Cleveley once more, the path briefly deserts the stream, then crosses a fence on the right and heads to the left of a garden to a metalled road, where you turn right. At the fork in the road by Cleveley Mill, take a bridleway on the left uphill to a gate further along the village street. Here turn left and follow the road out of the village until, just before you reach some farm buildings, a footpath sign indicates the route over a stile on the right. This path quickly regains the mill leat and follows it for a while.

23

The 17th-century pub at Church Enstone

5. When you reach the B4022, turn right up the road. After about 300 yards, a footpath sign on the left indicates our route leading diagonally uphill in the direction of a prominent horse chestnut tree just over the brow of the hill. A stile leads into a paddock, beyond which is a second stile beneath the horse chestnut tree. Follow the narrow path between a garden and paddock to its emergence among the cottages of Church Enstone. The lane dog-legs left and right and leads back to the main village street with the Crown Inn a welcoming sight beyond.

PLACES OF INTEREST NEARBY

The *Hoar Stone*, mentioned above, is by the Fulwell turn off the B4022, south of the A44.

At Woodstock, 7 miles south-east of Church Enstone along the A44, stands *Blenheim Palace* (see Walk 7), sitting amidst a huge park laid out by 'Capability' Brown, the centrepiece of which is a Grand Bridge over a lake formed by damming the very River Glyme featured in this walk. It is one of the top ten tourist attractions in Britain. However, what many paying visitors do not realise is that the park is criss-crossed by public footpaths that allow free access to most of the grounds to anybody with a modicum of map-reading skills.

CHADLINGTON AND DEAN: IN THE VALLEY OF THE EVENLODE

You are never far away from the sound of running water on this walk in the shadow of the former royal forest of Wychwood. The route follows Chadlington Brook from the very start at Mill End until close to its confluence with the Evenlode. After a short interlude in the Evenlode valley the path meets Coldron Brook, which it follows upstream to Dean Mill. A brief re-encounter with the Coldron Brook at an old clapper bridge enlivens the return leg.

The lasher (waterfall) at Mill End

Chadlington has an unusual layout – its five 'ends', Mill End, West End, East End, Brook End and Green End, are satellite hamlets surrounding the village centre. Mill End, where our walk starts, was obviously the site of a mill, and a 'lasher' (or waterfall) associated with it can still be seen. The delightful area around the site of the mill, where two streams meet, is open to the public under an environmental access scheme.

The middle part of the walk is along the Evenlode valley (though only with glimpses of the river). At this point the southern skyline is darkened by trees - the main remnant of Wychwood Forest, a former royal hunting forest and the largest area of ancient woodland remaining in Oxfordshire. Wychwood once covered a much larger area and there is now a scheme, the Wychwood Project, which aims to return some of the land within the original Norman boundaries (some 36 parishes) to woodland. Dean Common, encountered about halfway round this walk, is a case in point, where land used for gravel extraction has been newly planted with native species. Nearby Dean Grove is already wooded, and exhibits many coppice 'stools'. These are old trees, regularly harvested to produce a ring of fairly young trunks. It has been suggested that the oldest living thing in the British Isles may well be a coppice stool - some are over a thousand years old.

The Tite Inn takes its name from the 'tite', a continually running stream that flows beneath it and emerges into a trough beside the road. This was once the village water supply. The pub was originally built around 1600. In winter the log fire is a welcome sight, while in summer the garden and gravel terrace may prove more inviting. The pub serves a range of local real ales, and a wide selection of good food (including bar meals as well as a comprehensive restaurant menu). Local country cheeses are a speciality, and a range of good sandwiches in French bread will tempt the walker. Large groups are asked to call in advance, but booking is not normally necessary for bar meals. Telephone: 01608 676475; email titeinn@chadlington99.freeserve.co.uk

- **HOW TO GET THERE:** Leave the B4026 Charlbury–Chipping Norton road at Spelsbury and drive through Dean to Chadlington. Turn right at the village post office, then left into Mill End (signposted to Churchill). The pub is near the bottom of the valley on the right-hand side. Chadlington can also be reached from the west by following signposts from the A361 between Shipton-under-Wychwood and Chipping Norton.
- **PARKING:** Patrons may leave their cars in the car park of the Tite Inn (with permission) while they walk; there are a few parking places in the street opposite.
- **LENGTH OF THE WALK:** 5¼ miles. Maps: OS Landranger 164 Oxford, Chipping Norton and Bicester; OS Explorer 191 Banbury, Bicester and Chipping Norton (GR 324225).

THE WALK

1. From the car park of the Tite Inn follow the wide grassy footpath opposite, signposted to Brook End. This runs alongside the stream and past the lasher on the site of the old mill. Just beyond the lasher you can cross the stream by a bridge to explore the pretty area around its confluence with a sidestream. Our route, however, continues down the main stream, and crosses a little further down. It turns left and continues with the stream now on the left and the houses of West End at the top of the hill beyond. Over a stile is a tumbledown stone bridge beneath an oak tree, where generations of cattle have come to drink. At the end of this idyllic stretch you reach a lane in Brook End, where you turn left, still following the stream. When the stream passes under the road turn right, then left at a small green. This passes between cottages and then close by another to emerge in a field with the stream on the left. Admire, but do not cross, the pretty stone bridge in this field. Just short of the end of the field cross the stream again via a footbridge and turn right. You pass a farm ford on the right and a sewage works on the left. At the end of the field beyond the sewage works compound the path leaves the stream and heads to the left of a telegraph pole to a stile. Here you join the Oxfordshire Way and follow it left to the road.

2. Beyond the road our route continues through a gate along the Oxfordshire Way opposite. This path leads past a copse on the left, and then another on the right (and is joined by a minor stream briefly between the two). Beyond the second wood, the path drops to cross another small stream in a valley, then climbs to Dean Common on the other side. Turn right at the Dean Common information stone and walk to a footbridge over a dry stream. Then follow the left-hand edge of the field, with Dean Common through the hedge on your left. Turn right at the top of the field and walk along the edge of Dean Grove. At the beginning of the second field beyond the end of the wood, the path turns left through a kissing gate. Keep along the left-hand edge of this field to reach another kissing gate, where you turn left and walk across a further field to enter the woodland of Dean Grove. Follow the path through a couple more metal kissing gates as it runs through the wood, with Coldron Brook never far away to the right. When you reach a crossing path, turn right to leave the wood and enter a narrow meadow. Here turn left and walk northwards to a further kissing gate; this leads out into an open area. Keep along above the brook to the road, crossing a couple of stiles on the way.

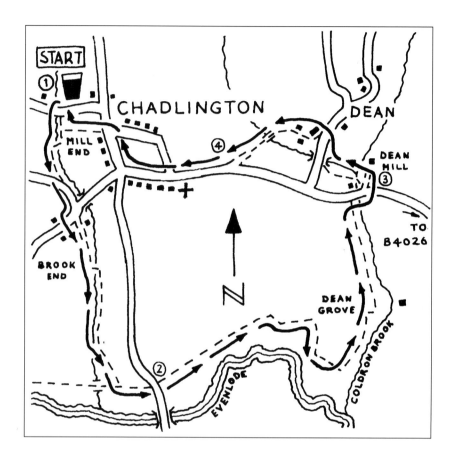

3. When you reach the road in Dean, turn right past an iron-roofed cottage with a squirrel on its weathervane, then turn left into the entrance to Dean Mill. Head left of the drive to a footbridge over the stream. Beyond a stile is a field full of ridge and furrow, with glimpses to some ponds on the right. Walk along the top of a wooded bank, then at the end of the field drop right to a stile in the far corner of the field. Turn right, crossing the stream, and walk uphill along the road to a row of cottages on the left. Double-back and walk in front of them, then swing right (passing to the right of a more modern house). Walk along the top of a field past a corrugated iron barn to a field gate. Here walk diagonally left downhill to the far corner of the field, where you cross the stream by a bridge. Walk along the hedge up the hillside beyond. Past a stile you enter a farm track, which you follow to the road.

The village pub at Mill End, Chadlington

4. Turn right past Langston House. Walk along the main street through East End, passing the church on the left (noticing its splendid gargoyles) and the tiny village school on the right. At the post office, turn right and walk past more modern housing until you reach the end of Church Street on the right. Here turn left over an old stone stile (older than the houses that surround it) into a path between two gardens that emerges into the access area. As long as the permitted access scheme continues to operate, it is probably preferable to walk straight down the hill to rejoin the stream below the old lasher and walk up the valley to return to the starting point the way you came, or to return to the pub via the road. (The right of way keeps to the right-hand edge of the field then, bizarrely, crosses a stile and passes directly across the back lawn of a private house and through a round brick archway to emerge shortly afterwards opposite the Tite Inn.)

PLACES OF INTEREST NEARBY
Knollbury is an ancient earthwork and possibly the site of a Roman camp, which can be reached by continuing west from Mill End; it lies about ½ mile from the Tite Inn on the right-hand side.

THE EVENLODE SOUTH
OF STONESFIELD

Stonesfield is set in lovely near-Cotswold countryside above the River Evenlode. The village was the centre of a localised stone-mining industry and the evidence of this activity adds an extra element of interest. Throw in a Roman road, a watermill, an ecologically interesting common and much more besides and you have the recipe for a fascinating walk.

The spot where Akeman Street crossed the Evenlode

The hard-wearing sandstone found around Stonesfield splits naturally into thin layers and, until the railways made the use of Welsh slate an economical proposition, it was much used for roofing buildings across a wide local area. At first the mining was opencast, but horizontal and then vertical mines (the deepest going down some 65 feet) were eventually dug to exploit the reserves of stone. 'Clamps' of stone thus extracted were buried under mounds of earth and damped down for the winter; frost split the rock into leaves, which were then cut to shape. Smaller, thinner slates were used at the tops of roofs, while the larger, thicker slates were reserved for the eaves. William Morris describes the Stonesfield slates on the roof of Kelmscott Manor (see Walk 13) as resembling the scales of a fish, and the famous Trout Inn at Wolvercote (Walk 9) is also Stonesfield-slated. The last mine closed in 1910, but signs of mining activities remain all around the village: there are disused pits and spoilheaps dotted around the fields north of the Evenlode. The parish magazine is still called *The Stonesfield Slate*.

The Roman road known as Akeman Street (which ran from Alcester near Bicester to Cirencester) forded the Evenlode just below the village in a pretty spot also visited by the Oxfordshire Way long-distance footpath. Upstream of this point the river winds attractively below a steep wooded bank, and is crossed by the single-track Oxford–Worcester railway line.

The White Horse was once three cottages and the barn, which now houses a skittle alley, was formerly used to store Stonesfield slates. There are open fireplaces in both bars, and some intriguing photographs of the stone mines on the walls. Hook Norton ales plus a guest beer are available for real ale enthusiasts. On the food front, the pub specialises in jacket potatoes, with other pub staples, sandwiches and light meals also available. There are at least four vegetarian options, and a children's menu. You are advised to book if you are bringing a large group or arriving at busy times such as summer weekends. Telephone: 01993 891604.

- **HOW TO GET THERE:** From the A44 a mile north-west of Woodstock, follow the B4437 towards Charlbury. At Ditchley Gate (an entrance to the Blenheim Estate) follow the unclassified road straight on; in the village follow the road right at the war memorial, then right again, to reach the White Horse at the top of Pond Hill.
- **PARKING:** Patrons may leave their cars in the car park of the White Horse (with permission) while they walk, or there is street parking nearby.
- **LENGTH OF THE WALK:** 4½ miles. Maps: OS Landranger 164 Oxford, Chipping Norton and Bicester; OS Explorer 180 Oxford, Witney and Woodstock (GR 392176).

THE WALK

1. From the White Horse walk down the hill past the Stonesfield Garage, until you reach a bus stop opposite a plaque commemorating the installation of waterworks to celebrate Queen Victoria's sixtieth

31

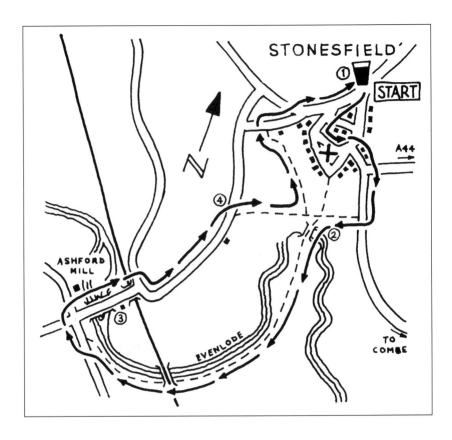

year on the throne. Here turn left into Boot Street. The Old Boot Inn and the Old Post Office both have Stonesfield slates on their roofs. At the Methodist Church keep left along the High Street. At the end of the street turn left past the Black Head pub, then right into Woodstock Road. Turn right by the war memorial into Combe Road, and pass the entrance to Stonesfield Manor with its short avenue of large beeches. Walk down the hill to the quaintly named Bagg's Bottom. Just short of the very bottom of the valley, turn right along a fieldside path. Notice the disused stone pits and old spoil-heaps in the field on your right, which continue in the second field. At the end of this field you cross a stile and swing right towards the Evenlode.

2. Cross the river via the footbridge and follow the path that leads straight ahead across the field. At the end of the field turn right through a gap in the hedge to follow the Evenlode upstream. The next stretch of path tends, maddeningly, to be overgrown in summer and muddy in winter, but do persist as the delights beyond will repay the effort. When the path reaches a wood the going gets rather easier as the path progresses delightfully among the coppices with the Evenlode on the right. Partway through the wood you pass under a railway arch (bearing the single track of the still-operative Oxford to Worcester line). Continue in similar vein beyond the railway until you walk through a young plantation and emerge in the road. Walk right for a few yards to the crossroads, then turn right and cross the river in front of Ashford Mill.

3. Walk up the hill past a few homes, including a barn conversion with an outcrop of bedrock in the road verge and the scant remains of a quarry in the garden, until you reach the oddly named Bridgefield Bridge over the railway. Beyond the bridge turn right and keep along the road.

4. About 100 yards beyond some farm buildings, turn right into a footpath that leads through a gate into Stonesfield Common. Follow the left-hand path across the common until, shortly before a stile at the far end of the field, you find a gate on the left which leads into a sunken way that drops down towards the footbridge you crossed earlier. Before you reach the bridge swing left, along a path that stays just within the trees with the attractive dry valley of Stockey Bottom on the right. Keep along the edge of the wood for rather more than ¼ mile (with more evidence of mining activities on the opposite side of the valley). Swing left along a track around the end of the wood, then right to a narrow and quiet lane by a farm building. Turn right and walk down the lane to the edge of Stonesfield. When you meet the main road, turn right and walk up the hill, crossing the Oxfordshire Way. Keep along the road (retracing your steps beyond Boot Street) to return to the starting point.

PLACES OF INTEREST NEARBY
The *Oxford Bus Museum* at Long Hanborough (with a car park, garden and teas) is to be found in the old BR yard next to Hanborough station, just off the A4095 between Woodstock and Witney. The purpose-built museum includes over 40 vehicles that saw local service, from horse-drawn trams to 1970s buses. Some of the exhibits are in working order and others are under restoration. For opening times and details of special events, call 01993 883617 (24-hour answering service).

WOODSTOCK AND BLENHEIM PALACE: THE VERSATILE GLYME

This short walk has two loops, so could be broken into two shorter circuits. The first loop of less than a mile takes you along the banks of the River Glyme through an area of overgrown watermeadows, now a nature reserve. The second and longer loop shows the Glyme in much less humble guise as, dammed to form a lake, it forms the centrepiece of the monumental landscaping of the Blenheim Palace estate. This is a good walk for wet conditions, as the paths are generally dry underfoot (except in the watermeadows, which can be inundated in winter).

The Grand Bridge, Blenheim

A true watermeadow is no haphazard, natural phenomenon. The waters that irrigated the land and annually inundated and refreshed it were carefully regimented: some ditches have gradients as shallow as 1½°. The richness of the resulting pasture was so valuable, and areas with the appropriate geography so rare, that even small suitable areas like that at Woodstock were cultivated in this way. An example of the skilful engineering employed can be seen partway along the first riverside stretch of this walk, where an irrigation channel runs in the opposite direction to the river from which the water has just flowed. The Woodstock Watermeadows are now maintained by the Town Council as a nature reserve and for quiet recreation. They obviously present a very different aspect to their original working appearance, having grown over with trees and scrub, and have been enhanced by the addition of ponds and careful management of the vegetation.

Beyond the main A44 road the Glyme abruptly changes its mood, from a humble working river to a majestic lake set in classical parkland. Blenheim Palace was built for John Churchill, Duke of Marlborough, in recognition of his victory over the French at Blenheim, a village on the Danube, in 1704. When originally built, the Grand Bridge spanned a rather insignificant canal between two lakes (Queen Elizabeth Island is a remnant of the original dam forming the upper lake). The famous landscape gardener Lancelot 'Capability' Brown later flooded the entire Glyme valley to form the extensive lake we see today. The plinth of the Column of Victory lists in exhaustive detail the exploits of the Duke and the terms of the endowment. Sir Winston Churchill was born at the Palace in 1874 and is buried at nearby Bladon.

The Black Prince pub is over 400 years old, and its name commemorates the fact that Edward, Prince of Wales and the son of Edward III, was born in Woodstock. The walls are hung with swords and a suit of armour stands in a corner. This free house has two large inglenook fireplaces with log fires in winter and four real ales are on offer. Food, which has a Mexican flavour, is served at lunchtime and in the evening. There is a delightful riverside garden, and dogs and children are welcome. Telephone: 01993 811530.

- **HOW TO GET THERE:** The Black Prince is on the right-hand side of the A44 as you head north-west out of Woodstock, before you leave the town at the bottom of a dip.
- **PARKING:** There is a good-sized car park at the Black Prince, which patrons are welcome to use while they walk; non-patrons will need to park elsewhere – try the residential areas to the right of the A44 further up the hill.
- **LENGTH OF THE WALK:** 3¼ miles. Maps: OS Landranger 164 Oxford, Chipping Norton and Bicester; OS Explorer 180 Oxford, Witney and Woodstock (GR 442170).

THE WALK

1. From the Black Prince, cross the Glyme then turn left over a footbridge into Woodstock Watermeadows. Keep along the Glyme, ignoring a footbridge on the right (this is our return route). After about ¼ mile, you reach a bridge over a sidestream near the far end of the reserve. Do not cross, but turn right just before the bridge. This leads to another footbridge over the same stream; once over, turn right and follow the parallel stream back towards the A44. At a footbridge just before you reach the main road, turn right to return to the Black Prince and the road.

2. To continue, cross the A44 and turn right. Notice the plaque on a house on the left, commemorating the location of the original Blenheim Orange apple tree. You can get away from the traffic slightly a little further up, where a side street on the left runs high above, but parallel to, the main road. At the end of this side street, opposite a former church, turn left to reach the kissing gate at the entrance to Blenheim Park.

3. Once through the gate follow the path as it slopes down towards the lake. When you reach the estate road, turn right and follow it parallel to the lakeside. You reach a cottage at the end of an arm of the lake; skirt round the cottage then when you have walked round three sides of it, strike off right (up the slope and away from the lake). The exact line of the public footpath is invisible on the ground – from the top of the slope aim about 75 yards left of the Column of Victory (though you will probably want to approach more closely to read the grandiloquent prose at its foot). Beyond the column, route-finding is rather easier as you follow a fence that joins you on your right. When the fence turns right, keep straight on to cross an estate road and head down a pretty dry valley through a grove of cedar trees. This leads eventually to another sinuous arm of the lake.

4. Turn left and walk along the stony track that follows the lake's edge. Eventually, you meet the main body of the lake (with glimpses to the Palace beyond) and the path swings left towards the Grand Bridge. As you near the bridge, the grassy public footpath leaves the obvious track and drops down to the right towards the water's edge and passes Fair Rosamund's Well, a spring enclosed in railings. The path then heads away from the lake briefly to join another estate road. Turn right as if

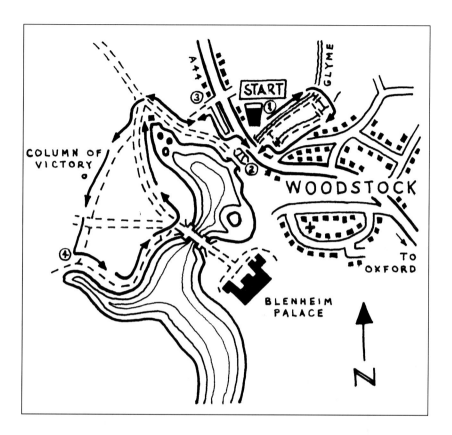

making to cross the lake. Before you reach the bridge turn left, almost doubling back on yourself, onto another estate road that leads you once more to the cottage at the end of the lake. (Alternatively, cross Grand Bridge and follow the estate road around the far side of Queen Pool, crossing the Glyme by a stone bridge.) Leave the park by the same gate you entered by. Return to the Black Prince by the same route as before.

PLACES OF INTEREST NEARBY
The *Oxfordshire County Museum* is housed in Fletcher's House, a fine 17th-century town house in Park Street, Woodstock, opposite the parish church. There are fascinating permanent galleries as well as a changing programme of temporary exhibitions, a coffee bar and a gift shop. Telephone: 01993 811456.

THE WINDRUSH VALLEY: MINSTER LOVELL TO CRAWLEY

This walk passes through fine scenery in a lovely part of the Windrush valley, and through two charming villages, but its highlight is undoubtedly the atmospheric riverside ruin of Minster Lovell Hall, close by the parish church of St Kenelm. The route is not strenuous, though flooding may render it impassable at very wet times of year and there is one short steep downward slope.

Minster Lovell Hall seen from the Windrush

Minster Lovell Hall was built in the first half of the 15th century for Lord William Lovell, whose family had held the manor for several generations before, but were to hold it for only two more after his death. His grandson Francis was the last and most famous of the Lovells. He became a prominent figure in the Yorkist court of Richard III and fought for him at Bosworth Field, the last of the Wars of the Roses, in 1485. He fled to France after the Lancastrian victory, but returned to fight in Lambert Simnel's rebellion. He may have died at the battle of Stoke (near Newark) in 1487, but a romantic legend has him escaping back to Minster Lovell and hiding in a cellar, fed by a faithful servant. The servant died, leaving Lovell to starve. In the early 18th century it is recorded that an underground room was discovered during the erection of a new chimney. Inside was said to have been the skeleton of a man seated at a desk with book, pen and paper to hand and his cap on the floor. Whether or not this ever happened, and whether the dead man was Francis Lovell, will probably never be known and the cellar has never been rediscovered.

In 1602 Sir Edward Coke, then Attorney General, purchased the manor, but his descendants built a new mansion at Holkham in Norfolk and Minster Lovell was eventually abandoned. The building was partly demolished in 1747, but there appears to have been little further deterioration beyond the end of the 18th century; the ruins have thus looked much the same for around 200 years.

After the Lovells and the Cokes, Minster Lovell might have been expected to lapse into obscurity, but it appears not to have lost its attraction to political figures. Douglas Jay, Economic Secretary to the Treasury in the Labour Government of 1945–50 and President of the Board of Trade, is buried in the churchyard of St Kenelm's church. Jack Straw, the Home Secretary at the time of writing, has a house in the village. The nearby village of Crawley has attracted national attention too, when a farm breeding cats for experimental purposes was eventually closed down after a protracted series of demonstrations by anti-vivisectionists.

The Old Swan at Minster Lovell is a splendid old building near the river, with the old well visible within the building. An inn and brewery was mentioned on the site in the Domesday Book, and Richard III is said to have stayed there during a visit to the Lovells. The pub is owned by the same company that runs the conference centre in the mill opposite, and patrons of the pub are invited to stroll around the immediate grounds of the mill. The Old Swan is open at lunchtime and in the evening during the week, and all day at weekends in summer. There is an extensive menu including bar meals, sandwiches, ploughman's lunches, fish and pasta. Well-behaved children and dogs are welcome (though dogs are excluded from the restaurant). Beers vary, but usually include a local real ale. Telephone: 01993 774441.

- **HOW TO GET THERE:** Old Minster Lovell is just north of the B4047, which runs between Witney and the A40 at Asthall Barrow near Burford. Descend from the B4047, cross the Windrush and the Old Swan is obvious by the junction with the main village street, near the conference centre.
- **PARKING:** The Old Swan's car park is often busy with visitors attending the conference centre, so you are advised to park at the public car park by the recreation ground, near the river.
- **LENGTH OF THE WALK:** 4¾ miles. Maps: OS Landranger 164 Oxford, Chipping Norton and Bicester; OS Explorer 180 Oxford, Witney and Woodstock (GR 318113).

THE WALK

1. From the Old Swan, walk up the main village street, passing a series of beautiful Cotswold cottages. Keep on past the entrance to Minster Lovell Hall and the church. Just beyond the last house, cross a stile on the right-hand side into a field (signposted to Crawley). Aim for a gate in the far corner of the field, just to the left of the distant chimney of Crawley Mill. Beyond this gate the path continues with a dry-stone wall on the left. At the end of the field cross a stone stile and follow the path ahead. This leads via a stile into the end of a sheep paddock in a dry valley, and then through a gate into a hedged lane. The variety of trees and shrubs suggests that this delightful route, on a bank above the flood meadows of the Windrush, is a thoroughfare of some antiquity. Eventually it emerges in a lane in Crawley, where you follow the road right to emerge at the village green by the war memorial and the Lamb Inn. Turn right and cross the Windrush by Crawley Bridge.

2. Opposite Crawley Mill take a bridleway on the left signposted to Witney. This leads pleasantly alongside a sidestream of the Windrush until you reach a gate within sight of New Mill. Here turn right and follow another bridleway uphill along the edge of a field to Dry Lane. Hill Grove Farm, where the cats were bred, is away to your left, but our route continues straight on across a narrow field and into a wood, unattractively named Maggots Grove. The path leads steeply down through the wood to emerge in the marshy watermeadows of the Windrush floodplain. Turn left; the path leads along the edge of the valley floor, with a wood above and to your left and a reedy sidestream to the right. Level with the end of the wood the path swings right over a stile and continues left along the near hedge to a gate and stile. Near a

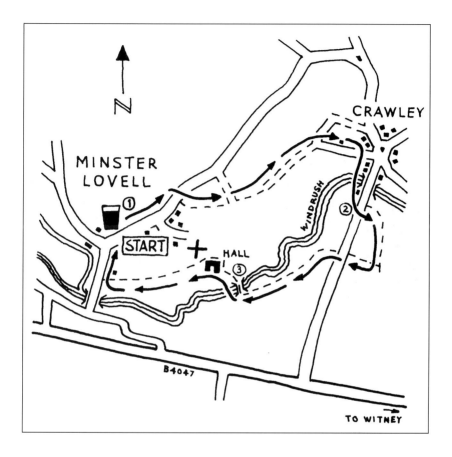

brick barn you enter an area of woodland close to the Windrush, and after a gate you reach the river. After this brief encounter (during which you cross two footbridges over small sidestreams), the path leads left, away from the river, with a reedy pond on the left and conifers to the right. This leads to a footbridge crossing the Windrush (this was once the main approach to Minster Lovell Hall, as suggested by the extensive bridgeworks).

3. Cross the river and walk towards a stile in front of the dramatic ruins. Enter the grounds of the Hall and walk around them to the right to enter the churchyard. The church is well worth looking around, but when you are ready to continue, leave the graveyard by a stone stile in the south-western corner, with the old fishponds to your left. In the far

41

The village of Crawley

left-hand corner of the next field is a stile and footbridge leading into another Windrush watermeadow. Turn right and walk along with the hedge on your right. Beyond two stiles you enter the recreation ground, named Wash Meadow because of its tendency to flood. Skirt the cricket pitch to the pavilion and car park (or pass through a gate on the right to regain the main village street and the Old Swan).

PLACES OF INTEREST NEARBY

Cogges Manor Farm Museum near Witney (widely signposted) is an excellent attraction for young and old alike. Adults will enjoy the insight into Edwardian country life, while children will probably prefer the old-fashioned breeds of animal kept in and around the farm. There are often 'hands-on' demonstrations of country cooking and other crafts. Telephone: 01993 772602 or see http://www.oxfordshire.gov.uk/default.htm.

GODSTOW TO SWINFORD: WATERMEADOWS OF THE THAMES

Above Oxford the Thames flows in a wide loop through an expanse of unspoilt meadowland, some of it of national importance for its plants and other wildlife. Within the loop is the wooded Wytham Hill, used for research by the University of Oxford. This walk samples these delights on this route from an ancient nunnery to one of only two remaining tollbridges on the Thames. The walk is longer than most in this book, but may be shortened by turning back at many points short of Swinford Bridge.

Eynsham Lock, with Wytham Woods in the background

A large proportion of the meadowland in this area, like Port Meadow to the south (see Walk 11), has never been ploughed. The meadows are managed traditionally to retain their ancient flora, which includes wildflowers such as great burnet and pepper saxifrage that cannot tolerate heavy grazing and are thus absent from Port Meadow.

Swinford was the site of a dangerous ford (the name indicating that it was shallow enough to allow the passage of swine) and later a ferry, which almost claimed the life of preacher John Wesley. The Earl of Abingdon purchased land on either side and obtained an Act of Parliament in 1767 allowing him to erect a bridge and collect tolls. The bridge opened two years later and tolls have been collected ever since. The bridge is still privately owned, and is one of only two tollbridges remaining on the Thames – the other is at Whitchurch (see Walk 20).

The Trout is a justly famous riverside pub overlooking the weirstream of the Thames at Godstow near Wolvercote. This stream was once the main navigation channel of the river. The inn is thought to have been built as a hospice associated with the Godstow Nunnery on the far side of the Thames. Stone from the Nunnery was used to extend the Trout, and the building is roofed with Stonesfield slates (see Walk 6). The interior is warm and welcoming, with three open fireplaces, stone-flagged floors and exposed beams. Such an attractive and historic pub was an obvious candidate for the attentions of local author Colin Dexter. A volume of his *Inspector Morse* series, entitled *The Wolvercote Tongue*, concerns the loss of an ancient jewel, which is eventually retrieved from the weir pool overlooked by the delightful terrace. The pub boasts a collection of Morse memorabilia, viewable on request.

The pub serves two real ales, eleven wines by the glass and a range of eight malt whiskies. Mulled wine and Pimms are popular specialities in winter and summer respectively. In winter, chestnuts are supplied free for roasting on the braziers on the terrace. There are separate lunch, evening and Sunday menus, as well as sandwiches, bar snacks and vegetarian options. Dogs are not welcome inside the pub, but can use the terrace (where they should be kept on a lead). The pub is open all day and food is served from noon until mid-evening. Telephone: 01865 302071.

- **HOW TO GET THERE:** The Trout can be reached via Wytham from the A34 north of Botley Interchange, or via Wolvercote from the A40 at its junction with the A44.
- **PARKING:** There is a large car park opposite the Trout for patrons (and a car park for the disabled alongside the pub). There is also a public car park not far away towards Wolvercote on the northern edge of Port Meadow.
- **LENGTH OF THE WALK:** 6¾ miles (may be shortened to 5¼ miles). Maps: OS Landranger 164 Oxford, Chipping Norton and Bicester; OS Explorer 180 Oxford, Witney and Woodstock (GR 485093).

THE WALK

1. Cross the narrow bridge beside the Trout, parts of which are only a little younger than Radcot Bridge, the oldest on the Thames (see Walk 13). Cross the second bridge and turn right onto the towpath along the main Thames navigation. This leads shortly to the A34 bridge, built in 1961 to cross the river and towpath. Once beyond this, cross a metalled track and walk diagonally over the field to a stile on the far side. A footbridge and further stile lead into another meadow; continue in the same general direction across a damp meadow with a varied flora until you reach the bridge by Wytham Mill. Here cross the Wytham Stream (a branch of the Thames), walk through the cluster of buildings and along the track to the road. The University Field Station is away to your right.

2. Cross the road and follow the fieldside path opposite as it slowly climbs towards Wytham Wood, with a hedge on your right. Just beyond a lone ash tree, cross to the opposite side of the hedge and continue in the same direction. At the end of the field swing right along the top edge, to a footbridge and stile. Beyond a further pasture, you reach an unmetalled lane, where you turn left towards the wood. On reaching the wood the path heads right, along the wood edge, with views of the river to your right and to Cassington church spire ahead. As it begins to descend, the path turns right to leave the edge of the wood, then at the end of the field it passes through a gateway then turns left, to regain the edge of Wytham Wood. The path follows the woodland edge, which gets closer and closer to the river. When the path reaches a gate and enters a pleasant stretch, with willows to the right and 'traditional' broad-leafed woodland on the left, you can easily swap to the towpath and turn for home. There will be plenty more opportunities to swap later as the two paths, our outward and return route, continue in close proximity almost as far as Swinford Bridge. Despite their closeness the two paths are very different in character, and both delightful.

3. The outward path leads through woodland to a kissing gate. It then enters a field where it winds between copses and clumps of scrub, always keeping well to the left. A footbridge over a stream leads to a rather more open field, and at the end of this field you are forced to turn right to join the towpath. To reach Swinford Bridge turn left and walk past Eynsham Lock, then head left to the foot of Swinford Bridge just before you pass under it. To visit the Talbot, a pleasant roadside

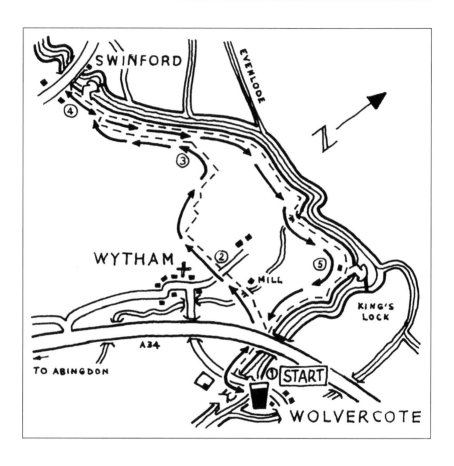

pub with a long association with the tollbridge, cross the bridge (free to pedestrians) and walk along the road for ½ mile and back (note that this extension is not included in the length of the walk quoted above).

4. When you have finished exploring the environs of Swinford Bridge, return along the towpath through the lock compound, and this time keep along the river. Notice the entry of the Wharf Stream on the left; this was once maintained as a navigable waterway to Eynsham. A little further on the woodland reaches right to the riverside; this is quite unusual and was allowed to occur only when the land next to the river is too steep, as here, to exploit as a watermeadow. As the river moves away from the woodland, the millstream of Cassington Mill can be seen entering the Thames on the far side. Slightly further downstream, a

The ruins of Godstow Nunnery

Thames Conservancy sign marks the confluence of the Evenlode and Thames. Half a mile or so beyond this, after a wide meander, the towpath crosses another millstream that leaves the river en route to Wytham Mill.

5. Eventually you reach King's Lock; here the river swings southwards and follows the metalled track encountered earlier as it approaches the roar of the A34 (you may also hear the A40 to the north). The chimney of Wolvercote Paper Mill is prominent. Beyond the A34, retrace your steps to return to the Trout, with perhaps a quick diversion to view the ruins of Godstow Nunnery and Godstow Lock beyond.

PLACES OF INTEREST NEARBY

Farmoor Reservoir, on the B4017 between Cumnor and Farmoor village, offers a variety of activities, including birdwatching, fly-fishing (day tickets available), windsurfing and sailing. There is also a countryside walk (if you have not walked far enough!) and a wetland reserve which can be overlooked from public footpaths. The warden's lodge and car park are at Gate 3; telephone: 01865 863033.

47

SHABBINGTON TO RYCOTE CHAPEL: THE SECRETIVE THAME

This farmland and riverside ramble features two historical sites set in pleasant countryside on the eastern edge of the county. First, across the fields from Shabbington, the route crosses the Thame via 17th-century Ickford Bridge. A little further, beyond the quiet hamlet of Albury, is Rycote Chapel, an architectural gem in the care of English Heritage. From Rycote the return is along one of the few stretches of footpath to follow the River Thame for a significant distance.

Ickford Bridge

This is border country. Ickford Bridge carries a stone dating it to 1685 and reading 'Here ends the county of Oxon; here beginneth the county of Bucks'. In fact the Old Fisherman and the first part of the walk are in Buckinghamshire, but the majority of the walk is south of the Thame and within Oxfordshire. Inter-county rivalries are felt strongly here. For over fifty years, on the first Friday in August, a tug-of-war has taken place between the villagers of Ickford and Tiddington on opposite sites of the county boundary. What draws the crowds is that the two teams assemble on opposite sides of the Thame and the losers get a soaking!

Rycote Chapel is maintained by English Heritage. The largely unaltered 15th-century building has a picturesque setting and exterior, but the real glory is inside. Dominating the interior are two roofed pews. One is traditionally said to have been constructed for a visit of Charles I and the other, used by the Norreys family, is a grandiose double-decker affair with a musicians' gallery. Both are extravagantly carved and painted, and there is much besides of interest within the building. The chapel is open (admission charge) from 2 pm to 6 pm on Fridays, Saturdays, Sundays and bank holidays from April to September. The adjacent Rycote Park (not open to the public) has a few remnants of the original 16th-century house, which was destroyed by fire in 1745.

The Old Fisherman stands right by the Thame on the site of an eel farm mentioned in the Domesday Book. At some point it was a mill, but it has been a public house for around 200 years. Sensitively renovated, its pleasantly light, beamed interior is adorned with signed photographs of celebrities who have visited. There is a full à la carte menu with daily specials and, appropriately given the pub's name and location, a fish board. Vegetarian options, home-made baguettes, light lunches and children's meals are also available. The pub is open all day every day and food is served at lunchtime and in the evening. You are advised to book if you wish to eat at weekends – telephone: 01844 201247. Please note that dogs are not welcome.

- **HOW TO GET THERE:** From junction 8 of the M40 follow signposts towards Thame through Tiddington on the A418 until you reach the hamlet of North Weston. Turn left, and the Old Fisherman is beyond the bridge over the River Thame about a mile north of the main road.
- **PARKING:** The Old Fisherman has ample parking which patrons are welcome to use while they walk.
- **LENGTH OF THE WALK:** 5 miles. Maps: OS Landranger 164 Oxford, Chipping Norton and Bicester or 165 Aylesbury and Leighton Buzzard, Thame and Berkhamsted; OS Explorer 180 Oxford, Witney and Woodstock (GR 667065).

THE WALK

1. Head away from the Old Fisherman along the road up the hill towards Shabbington village. Turn left into the churchyard and walk behind the church to a stile into a field, and then head right towards the buildings of Franklin's Farm. To the right of a farm bungalow is a stile into a paddock, which leads to a second and then a third stile. Beyond the paddocks, head half-left, aiming just to the left of a couple of barns on the far side of the field. By the barns is a double stile and a footbridge; beyond this aim diagonally left towards a gap in the hedge (crossing a farm track partway across). Once through the gap, aim for a kissing gate in the projecting corner of the next field. Keep on in the same direction to a footbridge over a stream, then turn left and walk along with the stream on your left. A footbridge carries you over a

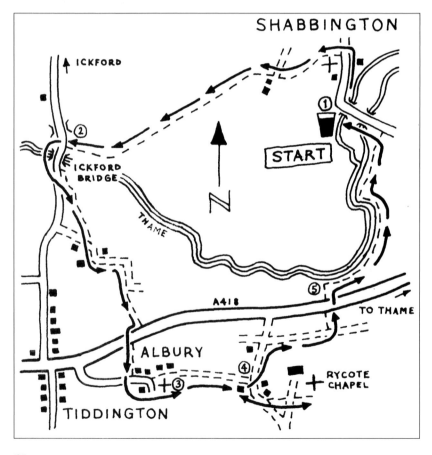

The pub at the start of the walk

damp patch in the corner of the field, from where you walk straight across the next field to a stile close to the river. Follow the river downstream to a stile between Ickford Bridge and the evocatively named Whirlpool Arch – there is no sign of a whirlpool in the tranquil pond it now spans!

2. Turn left to cross Ickford Bridge, noting the boundary marker on the eastern parapet. Beyond the bridge look out for a footbridge and a stile into the belt of trees on your left. Follow the belt of trees then, when it broadens out at a fence, skirt round to the left of the trees. At the rear of the copse there is a stile by a gate, at which point swing left, aiming between a large barn and a modern house to its left. This will take you to a concrete farm track – cross a gate (sometimes padlocked) then turn left through another gate into a pleasant green lane. Follow this lane when it turns right. Near the end of the lane, a stile and gate on the right-hand side lead out into a field. Turn left and walk along the hedge to emerge in a layby on the A418. Turn right and walk quickly but carefully along the main road for about 100 yards. Look out for a gate beneath an oak tree on the opposite side. (This is easily overlooked; if you miss it and reach the turning to Albury, simply

51

follow the Albury lane.) If you do manage to find the gate, pass through it into a thistly field to the disused railway, where a footbridge leads across a damp patch to a stile. Beyond this walk up the field, to the right of a house, to the lane in Albury. Turn left.

3. Enter the churchyard and seek out a kissing gate in the far left-hand corner, by farm buildings that have been converted into offices. Turn right and pass a barn (still in agricultural use). Follow the track ahead, with good views to the left over the Thame valley to the hilltop villages of Brill and Long Crendon, both in Buckinghamshire, and to Thame parish church ahead of you. When you reach Home Farm walk past the house and turn right. This track winds through the farm to the entrance to another house on the left; here the track heads slightly right; leave it to cross to a stile directly opposite, then cross another stile into the grounds of Rycote Park to visit the chapel. Return to Home Farm by the same route.

4. Walk down the drive of Home Farm towards the main road once more. Just beyond a house, turn right onto a farm track along the line of the old railway. You pass the end of a wood on the right, then continue to the beginning of another wood, this time to the left of the railway line. Turn left here down some steps and follow the wood edge to the main road. Follow the path almost directly opposite which leads very shortly to the River Thame. Turn right.

5. Follow the river closely for a pleasant mile. When you reach the road near your starting point, turn left and cross three bridges to return to the pub.

PLACES OF INTEREST NEARBY
Waterperry Horticultural Centre – 'a gardener's garden' which surrounds Waterperry House and the adjoining part-Saxon church – can be reached from the A40 at Wheatley, or from Shabbington via Worminghall. A huge variety of plants, many rare and unusual, can be enjoyed in beautifully designed and dynamically evolving plantings. There is also an art and crafts gallery, a garden centre and shop, and a teashop and restaurant. Telephone: 01844 339254.

BINSEY AND THE WATERWAYS OF OXFORD

The walk follows the main Thames navigation, a couple of Oxford's many Thames sidestreams and an interesting stretch of the Oxford Canal. It passes close to the centre of Oxford but is busy only for a short stretch; there are no fewer than six pubs en route and many more a short distance away.

Isis Lock

This walk begins at Binsey, a hamlet consisting of a farm, the Perch pub and a row of pretty cottages (and an isolated church nearly ½ mile away at the end of Binsey Lane). Beyond the river is the historic expanse of Port Meadow, an important botanical site (being the last remaining site for the endangered creeping marshwort). It floods every winter and at such times attracts large numbers of wading birds and ducks.

This stretch of the Oxford Canal is industrial in places (particularly the former Lucy's Ironworks) but is nonetheless a valuable green artery leading into the centre of the city, with a colourful year-round contingent of houseboats. The present-day canal stops short of the original terminus, a canal basin now occupied by Worcester Street car park.

Castle Mill Stream, which runs through the western part of the city centre, was once the main Thames navigation. It flows right by the Norman tower of Oxford Castle, which is within the perimeter of the former Oxford prison. The weir by the tower was the site of the watermill that gives the stream its name. A short distance downstream from the weir, Oxford's most mysterious waterway leaves the Castle Mill Stream through a locked sluice. This is the Trill Mill Stream, which flows through a tunnel beneath the streets of Oxford and emerges near the St Aldates entrance to Christ Church Meadow.

Only a mile from busy and unlovely Botley Road, the Perch at Binsey is a well-known local hostelry famed for its beautiful, remote-seeming location and its lovely garden. The thatched 17th-century inn serves a wide range of good food, with daily changing specials, a specialist fish menu and a variety of baguettes and light meals. In summer there is a daily barbecue and occasional spit roasts. Four real ales are available, including a guest beer, and a good selection of wines by the glass. In the winter mulled wine is a favourite, and in the summer the seasonal choice changes to Pimms or fruit cocktails. Food is served at lunchtime and every evening except Sunday and the pub is open all day in summer. Please book in advance if arriving with a large group – telephone 01865 240386. Dog-owners are asked to keep to the garden or the heated and covered terrace.

- **HOW TO GET THERE:** Binsey is accessed by car from A420 Botley Road; if travelling towards the city centre, look out for the sign to Binsey Lane on the left-hand side. Walkers using public transport should start from Folly Bridge, a short walk from the city centre, or from Hythe Bridge Street or Osney Bridge, which are close to Oxford Station.
- **PARKING:** Patrons may park in the Perch car park (with permission) while they walk; there are a small number of parking spaces in the road for non-patrons, but please obey any 'no parking' notices.
- **LENGTH OF THE WALK:** 5 miles. Maps: OS Landranger 164 Oxford, Chipping Norton and Bicester; OS Explorer 180 Oxford, Witney and Woodstock (GR 493077).

THE WALK

1. From the Perch car park, walk towards the road then turn left by the cattle grid and walk down the track signposted to Bossom's Boatyard.

When you reach the riverbank, with Port Meadow ahead of you on the far bank, turn right and walk down towards the boatyard. Keep to the riverside path rather than entering the boatyard. This takes you to the foot of Rainbow Bridge, by which you cross the main navigation. On the far side, turn right, then at the next bridge turn left to cross the boatyard basin and reach Port Meadow. Turn right and follow the back stream ('Willow Walk'), unless the path here is flooded, in which case the path leading across the meadow ends up in the same place, a small car park at the end of Walton Well Road. Turn right and cross the railway bridge, and then a sidestream. Opposite the entrance to the new Rutherway development, and just before the canal bridge, take the path that slopes down under a bridge to the canal towpath.

2. Turn right and walk down the towpath past Lucy's Ironworks and then some new flats. After this, the canal environs become greener and more pleasant. Pass under a footbridge, and on the far bank you pass the boatyards of Jericho in the shadow of St Barnabas' church. Beyond this you reach Isis Lock (known to locals as Louse Lock, for unknown reasons); cross bridge number 243 (built 1796) and continue along the towpath. Look out on the right-hand side for a gate in the stone wall beyond the Castle Mill Stream; this is the water gate of Rewley Abbey, the only remnant of this important ecclesiastical house. Beyond the canal on your left, at more-or-less the same point, you may be able to glimpse the lake in the grounds of Worcester College.

3. When you reach busy Hythe Bridge Street, cross over and follow the Mill Stream Walk, which continues on the opposite bank. This leads shortly to Park End Street, which you cross and continue in the same direction along the Mill Stream. The next road you encounter is St Thomas Street, at the quaintly named Quaking Bridge. Keep straight on, passing the weir below the Castle tower and the forbidding walls of the former prison. Cross the Mill Stream then, just before the junction with Paradise Square and the Jolly Farmers pub, turn right following the Mill Stream Walk signpost. This leads to the left of the Old Malthouse building into the grounds of Oxford College of Further Education. The sluice leading into the Trill Mill Stream culvert is in a small garden area to your right. Just before you reach the main college buildings, turn left, then almost immediately right to cut across the pay-and-display car park to reach Thames Street by the bridge over the Mill Stream. Do not cross the bridge, but cross the road carefully to find a

further path opposite, which leads alongside the stream with modern housing on the left. This leads you the confluence of the Castle Mill Stream and the River Thames; swing left and pass under the brick arch of the so-called Gas, Light and Coke Bridge. This bridge, built in 1886, connected the city to the former gasworks on the far bank (now Grandpont Nature Park) and carried the huge gas mains, as well as a single-track railway and a narrow road. Now it is merely a rather ornate and incongruous footbridge. (You can cut ½ mile or so off the route here by crossing the bridge and turning right along the towpath on the far bank.) Otherwise, follow the towpath downstream. You pass under a metal footbridge, then through a metal gate that (perhaps deliberately) suggests that the path is private; this is not the case. Beyond a second gate, just as you reach Folly Bridge, the path swings left behind the tollhouse to reach the Abingdon road. Turn right to cross Folly Bridge and then, opposite the new Graduate Centre of Hertford College, turn right again and cross a footbridge to join the towpath on the opposite bank. Keep along the river, passing under the metal footbridge again to return to the Gas, Light and Coke Bridge.

4. Keep on along the towpath with Grandpont Nature Reserve on your left, passing the ship-like building housing Oxford Ice Rink beyond the river on the right. Pass under a railway bridge and cross a footbridge over the Bulstake Stream. A little further on, across a grey-painted footbridge, you reach Osney Lock, in the shadow of the gaunt brick ruin of Osney Mill. Beyond the weir bridge and a third footbridge you reach Osney Island and the Waterman's Arms. Keep on along the towpath, passing the former power station on the opposite bank. This leads you to Osney Bridge, often considered the divide between the Upper and Lower Thames (particularly because its low beam, only 7'6" above water level, prevents many larger craft from going any further). Cross a sidestream by a footbridge to reach Botley Road.

5. Cross carefully, turn right and cross the bridge. The towpath continues on the opposite bank, which has been newly restored using 'environmentally friendly' willow stakes. This short stretch between houses and allotments leads to an arched bridge over a sidestream (which connects to the canal at Isis Lock). Keep on along the towpath beyond the bridge. You are now on Fiddler's Island, presumably so called because of the vague resemblance of its shape to a violin bow. When you come to Medley, retrace your steps over Rainbow Bridge and past the boatyard. To reach the Perch, by way of variation instead of following the track back to Binsey, keep along the towpath then shortly take a footpath on the left which leads to the pub garden.

PLACES OF INTEREST NEARBY

There are obviously so many things to do in Oxford that to list a selection seems superfluous. One recommended activity, however, is to take an hour-long guided tour of the *Castle Mound* (during which you get an unusual view of Oxford, and an opportunity to visit the mysterious well chamber within the mound). Telephone: 01865 815559.

SANDFORD-ON-THAMES AND KENNINGTON: THE RIVER SOUTH OF OXFORD

The villages of Sandford and Kennington straddle the Thames just south of Oxford. This short walk begins at busy Sandford Lock, between the two villages. The middle section skirts ancient Bagley Wood in a pleasant shady interlude, and the return from Kennington village is along a popular stretch of the Thames, much travelled by steamers from Oxford and other pleasure craft. The walk is mainly level with no serious hills or other obstacles, though parts may be muddy after wet weather.

The King's Arms at Sandford Lock

Sandford Lock was one of the first three pound locks to be built on the Thames and is still the deepest, with a fall of over 8 feet in times of low water. Parts of the stonework from the original lock of 1632 are still on view beside the modern lock.

58

The sinuous weirstream alongside the lock cut is known as Fiddler's Elbow and thunders over Sandford Lasher, an impressive sight in spate. The potential of such a weight of water would obviously have attracted millwrights in the days of waterpower, and there were at least three mills on this reach at one time, the earliest documented in a charter of 1170. The only one that survives today is Sandford Mill below the lock. It operated as a paper mill from 1816 until its closure in 1982, and has since been converted into luxury housing.

Kennington village was for much of its history a satellite of Radley, but has now outgrown its parent. In the centre among the modern housing are a few older buildings, including the Victorian church of St Swithun, a few thatched cottages and old barns, and the 16th-century manor house. Kennington residents apparently have an ancient right to wander in Bagley Wood (owned by St John's College). This enviable privilege is not available to the casual visitor, but this walk makes use of an attractive (and universally applicable!) right of way to give a glimpse of this large woodland area.

The King's Arms at Sandford Lock has an enviable position which it exploits to the full, with its flower-hung frontage facing directly onto the lockside and large riverside garden shaded by a venerable horse chestnut tree. The pub is open all day, summer and winter, with a range of food available right through from noon until mid-evening. Children are welcome (and there is play equipment indoors and out), but dogs are restricted to the garden. Large parties wishing to eat are asked to notify the pub in advance. Telephone: 01865 777095.

- **HOW TO GET THERE:** The start of the walk can be reached by car from either side of the river. From the A4074, follow signs to Sandford and in the village turn left into Church Road and continue to its end. From Abingdon, follow signs through Radley to Kennington, then just as you enter the village, take a narrow no through road (Sandford Lane) on the right, which leads to the riverside. Park and cross the river via a large footbridge and the lock gates.
- **PARKING:** On the Sandford side, there is a large car park at the King's Arms for patrons only (please ask if you want to leave your car while you walk) and limited street parking some distance away elsewhere in the village; on the Kennington side there is ample free parking.
- **LENGTH OF THE WALK:** 3½ miles. Maps: OS Landranger 164 Oxford, Chipping Norton and Bicester; OS Explorer 180 Oxford, Witney and Woodstock (GR 532013).

THE WALK

1. From the riverside entrance to the King's Arms cross the footbridge over the first limb of the river, just above the point where the water disappears beneath the mill building. Cross the lock via the lower set of gates, and follow the path left, to go over the weir cut by a wide, concrete footbridge. If you parked on the Kennington side of the river, this is your starting point. Follow the narrow lane straight on, away from the river. The pavement here is raised high above the road, so as to remain passable in times of flooding. The road leads under a narrow railway bridge, immediately beyond which take a narrow path on the left, which leads into the corner of a field. Follow the field edge adjacent to the railway until you reach a footpath sign about halfway along the field. Here turn half-right and follow a path diagonally across the field. At the far side this passes through a wide gap in a hedge and then leads right along the hedge for a short distance to the Kennington road.

2. Cross over and turn left, then shortly afterwards turn right along a road signposted to Bayworth and Sunningwell, which skirts a wooded mobile home site and continues along the edge of the wood. Just before the end of the wood, take a shady path that leads away to the right (signposted to Kennington). This path leads attractively just inside the woodland edge for slightly over ¼ mile to a stream, which is crossed by a footbridge. The path leads on, now in a pleasant field (Kennington Memorial Field) with woodland on your left, to a gate into a sports ground. Keep along the left-hand edge to a staggered gate in the corner. This path leads between gardens to Bagley Wood Road. Cross over into a gravel drive to the right of the lane opposite; this leads between modern houses and at its end a path continues in the same direction with a wall on the left. The path emerges into a narrow lane, which you follow to the right until it emerges in the centre of Kennington, by the war memorial opposite the church.

3. Turn left and walk along the main village street, past thatched cottages and barns, until a narrow hedged path leads off to the right, beside the Tandem pub. The path crosses the railway by a footbridge, and then leads over a cycle path (part of the National Cycle Network) and a metal footbridge into a watermeadow. Keep on in the same direction to reach the riverbank, and turn right.

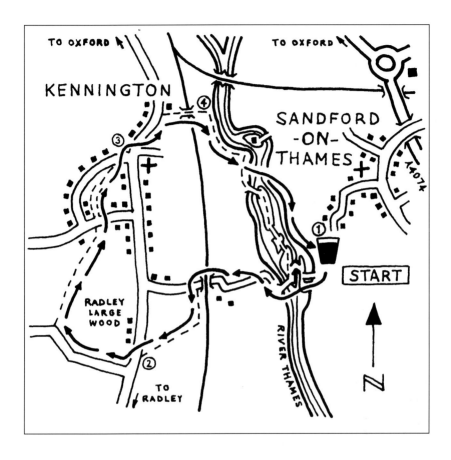

4. The path, which may be boggy in places, meanders around and beyond the attractive house on Rose Isle and then, after a short hedged stretch, crosses a low grey footbridge over a sidestream known as Fiddler's Elbow. The path then leads along a series of islands joined by bridges and weirs, until you reach Sandford Lock. Recross the downstream lock gates to return to the King's Arms.

PLACES OF INTEREST NEARBY
Nuneham Courtenay, not far south of Sandford on the A4074, is an interesting estate village. *Nuneham Courtenay Arboretum* is an outpost of the Oxford Botanic Garden and is normally open to the public from May to October.

61

ALONG THE THAMES: KELMSCOTT MANOR TO RADCOT BRIDGE

This walk in the remote Upper Thames Valley has two main highlights. The starting point is Kelmscott village, an unspoiled Cotswold stone village whose famous Manor House was home to the Victorian poet, painter, craftsman and socialist writer William Morris. From Kelmscott we cross the Thames and make our way via the isolated hamlet and church of Eaton Hastings to Radcot Bridge, the oldest surviving bridge on the whole of the River Thames. The return journey is a pleasant stroll along the willow-hung Thames towpath.

The Thames at Radcot

Kelmscott is famous as the home of William Morris, who lived at the Manor House for quarter of a century from 1871 and published his *News from Nowhere*. The unspoiled 16th-century building is graced by Morris's art and crafts, and works by Rossetti, Burne-Jones and others of his Pre-Raphaelite circle. The house and grounds are open to the public on Wednesday afternoons, and some Saturday afternoons, in summer (telephone 01367 252486). Morris is buried at the parish church of St George which, like many others, was saved from over-enthusiastic Victorian restoration by his influence.

Radcot, for such a tiny place, has more than its fair share of history. Only from Radcot Bridge does Newbridge, a few miles downstream and a scant half-century younger, seem accurately named. The first official record of a bridge at Radcot is in the Patent Rolls of King John (1208/9) but the fact that this is a reference to repairs, and other archaeological evidence, suggests that the bridge was actually built not long after 1150. Slightly older still is The Garrison, or Matilda's Castle, a large earthwork immediately to the north-west of the bridge.

The central arch of the bridge, as is obvious from its rounded shape, was built later than the others, after the bridge was deliberately damaged during an encounter between the Barons and Richard II's troops in 1387. There were also at least four skirmishes here during the Civil War, with fatalities on each occasion. Even as late as the 20th century, First World War troops trained here on bicycle manoeuvres, amusingly described in the booklet *Radcot and its Bridge*, available from the Swan Inn.

In more peaceful times, Radcot was an important link in the world of commerce. Stone quarried at Taynton and Burford was brought to the complex of wharves (evidence of which can still be seen by the expert eye) for shipment to London. Sir Christopher Wren used Oxfordshire stone shipped from Radcot in the building of the new St Paul's Cathedral after the Great Fire of London. There are said to be large blocks of stone still lying in the fields near the site of the medieval wharves.

The Plough Inn at Kelmscott is a pretty whitewashed building of 1631 by the stump of a medieval cross. Inside this free house, the front bar with its original flagstones, oak beams and open fireplace is always a welcoming sight and the comfortable back rooms house dining tables, where you can choose from five or six daily specials or from the comprehensive menu (which always includes several vegetarian options). Light meals such as filled baguettes or tortillas are also available, and there is a separate child's menu. Two real ales are always on tap, and sloe wine is something of a speciality. The pub is open all day seven days a week during the summer, and normal pub hours in winter. Food is served at lunchtime and in the evenings. You are advised to book if you wish to eat at weekends, particularly in summer. Telephone: 01367 253543; email ploughk@waitrose.com. Accommodation is available.

The Swan Inn at Radcot, conveniently placed for a mid-walk drink, has a well-kept riverside garden and a cosy interior decorated with magnificent fishing trophies caught locally.

- **HOW TO GET THERE:** Kelmscott is reached via minor roads from the A4095 between Clanfield and Faringdon. Take the turning north of Radcot Bridge signposted to Langford and Kelmscott. Ignore two right-hand turnings to Grafton and Langford, then turn left at a crossroads. Follow the road round to the right at the first junction, then take the left-hand turning into the village to reach the Plough.
- **PARKING:** There is limited parking at the Plough Inn (available only to patrons, and please ask permission before leaving your car while you walk). Alternatively, parking should be possible nearby in the village.
- **LENGTH OF THE WALK:** 6½ miles. Maps: OS Landranger 163 Cheltenham and Cirencester, Stow-on-the-Wold; OS Explorer 170 Abingdon, Wantage and Vale of White Horse (GR 249991).

THE WALK

1. Follow the driveway in front of the Plough to the left, away from the village street. Our path skirts right of a garden and follows a green lane across fields. At the end of the green lane (sometimes rather overgrown) turn abruptly left and walk along the left-hand edge of a field to a footbridge over a minor sidestream of the Thames. On reaching the river, cross by the footbridge. There was once a weir here, Hart's Weir (the last flash lock on the Thames), and more recently it was the site of the Anchor, a popular pub until it was tragically destroyed in a fire in 1980 when three people lost their lives. Only a single outbuilding remains. Follow a path to the left over a further bridge and along another reedy sidestream, crossing a number of stiles. There are views to the south to Buscot House in its wooded surroundings.

2. As you approach a lonely cottage, aim uphill and slightly to the right of it, to a stile. In the field beyond keep close to the left-hand edge, above the steeply wooded riverbank. The next field leads you in front of Rhodes Farm, with its unusual weathervane. Crossing a further field brings you out in the lane near Eaton Hastings church. Walk straight on, past the church, then negotiate a stile to the right of the entrance to Eaton Hastings House. This leads to Lower Farm.

3. Cross in front of the farmhouse, climb over a stile at the foot of a

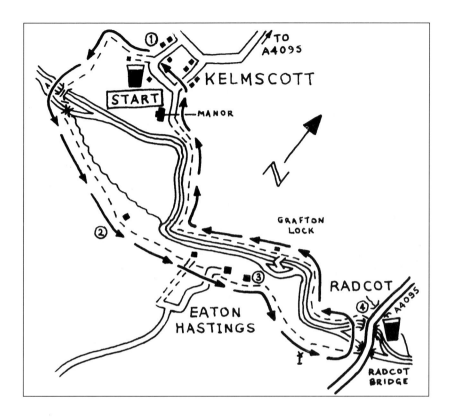

telegraph pole then skirt around to the right-hand side of the farm buildings. From the rear of the farm, head slightly left to a stile and footbridge beneath a willow tree. Continue in a similar direction to another double stile and footbridge. Keep left of the reedy pond in the next field, which marks the site of a disused pit, to a metal stile in the far left-hand corner. A series of stiles leads towards the prominent wind-pump below Camden Farm; our route leads just to the left of the wind-pump. A short wooded stretch by a pond leads to yet another stile. The path drifts vaguely diagonally across a long, narrow field with the river along its left-hand edge until you reach Radcot Bridge. Turn left and cross the bridge.

4. Cross the main navigation via the 'Canal Bridge' (comparatively modern at just over 200 years old!) and, unless you are intending to visit the Swan Inn, take the towpath to the left on the far bank. Beyond

Radcot Bridge, the oldest on the Thames

a footbridge, the earthworks of The Garrison are clearly visible to your right. From here directions are superfluous for the next 3 miles, as the paths stick rigidly to the riverbank, passing pretty Grafton Lock and with distant southward views to Faringdon and its Folly, until you reach the gravelly track to Kelmscott. Here leave the river and follow the track into the village. Notice the rare stone slab wall as you approach the Manor. When you reach the main village street in Kelmscott, turn left to return to the Plough; partway along on the left don't overlook the relief of William Morris set into the wall of Morris Cottages, which were built at the expense of Morris's widow as a memorial to him.

PLACES OF INTEREST NEARBY
Buscot House is an 18th-century stately home administered by Lord Faringdon on behalf of the National Trust. Its star attraction is the Faringdon collection of paintings and furniture. The grounds feature a water garden, woodland, several lakes and one of Oxfordshire's few heronries. Telephone: 01367 240786. To reach Buscot, turn left out of Kelmscott, then left again on the A417 over St John's Bridge, Lechlade (above the first lock on the Thames, itself worth a visit with its famous reclining statue of Father Thames).

TADPOLE BRIDGE AND UPPER THAMES WATERMEADOWS

This is a lonely walk in the misty watermeadows of the Upper Thames. The area is rich in wildlife: in spring and early summer the meadows are haunted by the eerie calls of curlew and the drumming of snipe. Chimney Meadow is a National Nature Reserve, a precious 50-hectare remnant of the unimproved grassland that was once common along the Thames and which supports a specialised and fragile flora and fauna. Boots and long trousers are recommended for this route.

The paddle weir at Rushey Lock

Tadpole has been described as 'the smallest hamlet in the country'. A cottage once stood opposite the Trout Inn but is now in ruins, so only the pub and bridge remain. There was formerly a coal wharf here.

The three river crossings encountered on this walk are all of interest. Tadpole Bridge was built of Taynton stone in 1802. A mile or so upstream at Rushey Lock the route crosses a 'paddle weir', one of very few such weirs remaining on the Thames. The water is controlled by introducing baffles known as 'paddles' into the flow. The final river crossing, the attractive and steep wooden footbridge at Tenfoot Bridge, is thought to get its name from the weir it replaced, which was presumably ten feet wide.

Chimney Meadow lies to the north of the river between Tadpole and Tenfoot Bridge. Some 50 hectares in extent, it constitutes a National Nature Reserve (the highest tier of nature reserve designation), and is managed by the local wildlife trust BBOWT. To protect nesting birds (which include snipe, curlew and redshank, all rare breeders in this county) and rare plants from disturbance there is no public access to the meadow, which should be viewed from the towpath only. Although much of the wildlife value was lost after the 1848 Enclosure Act and the 1866 Drainage Act, the area still supports rare plants including snakes-head fritillary, green-winged orchid, yellow rattle and adder's tongue, all typical plants of neutral hay meadow, a rare habitat these days.

The Trout Inn at Tadpole Bridge is a popular pub, despite its isolated location, and is frequently visited by Thames Path walkers. A past landlord was one Mr Herring, and a sign above the door once famously read 'The Trout, kept by A. Herring'. The restaurant-style menu always includes at least three vegetarian options; booking is advisable if you wish to eat. The regular real ales are Archers and Fuller's London Pride, supplemented by one guest beer in the winter and two in summer. There is a large garden stretching down to the riverside, with public moorings and 2 miles of fishing rights. Well-behaved children and dogs are welcome. The pub is open daily (except Sunday evenings in winter) and food is served at lunchtime and every evening except Sunday. Telephone: 01367 870382; http://www.troutinn.co.uk.

- **HOW TO GET THERE:** Leave the A420 Oxford–Faringdon road west of Buckland, signposted to Bampton. Tadpole Bridge is about 1½ miles from the main road. It is a similar distance from the Buckland turn off the B4449 at Bampton.
- **PARKING:** Patrons are welcome to leave their cars in the pub car park while they walk; there is room for a few cars in a layby on the other side of the bridge.
- **LENGTH OF THE WALK:** 5¾ miles. Maps: OS Landranger 164 Oxford, Chipping Norton and Bicester; OS Explorer 180 Oxford, Witney and Woodstock and 170 Abingdon, Wantage and Vale of White Horse (GR 335004).

THE WALK

NB: Be prepared for mud on much of this route – and flooding in times of high water.

1. Turn right out of the Trout Inn and cross Tadpole Bridge. Follow the towpath to the left (with a Thames Walk signpost indicating 4 miles to Radcot). The towpath joins the metalled track, which leads you to Rushey Lock after about a mile. Partway along you pass a Second World War pillbox. When you reach the lock, cross via the lower set of gates and walk past the lock-keeper's cottage.

2. Beyond the cottage, cross the weir via a permitted path, and notice the rack of paddles that are used to adjust the flow through the weir. The path heads briefly left alongside the weir pool to a grassy area sometimes used as a fishermen's car park, where you turn right, away from the river, to a stile beneath a willow tree and concealed behind a bank. This leads you into the corner of a field, where you follow the right-hand edge. At the end of the field you cross a footbridge, beyond which you again keep to the right-hand edge of the field towards Buckland Marsh Farm. The path is fenced as it passes two paddocks by the farm, where it can become rather nettly. Beyond this stretch continue in the same direction until you pass between the end of a hedge and the last cottage of Carswell Marsh; here turn left along the hedge.

3. Cross a farm track and keep in the same direction, with the steep wooded slope of Marriage Hill to your right. At the end of the field, walk straight across the next field, aiming for a metal gate. Beyond the gate the path leads along the edge of a field with a hedge on the right, to the road. Turn left and walk through the hamlet of Buckland Marsh. Just beyond a bridge over a Thames sidestream, turn right through a gateway and return to the stream. Follow this sidestream for about 1½ miles, with views on the right to Buckland House and village. You pass a track leading down from Rectory Farm and shortly afterwards turn left at a footpath sign down a hedged track to Tenfoot Bridge.

4. Cross the steep wooden footbridge over the Thames. Ahead are the splendid marshy fields of Chimney Meadow. Turn left along the towpath, which passes between some blackthorn shrubs and is sometimes rather churned up by the cattle. Follow the river round a series of meanders to a grey-painted gate at the end of the Chimney

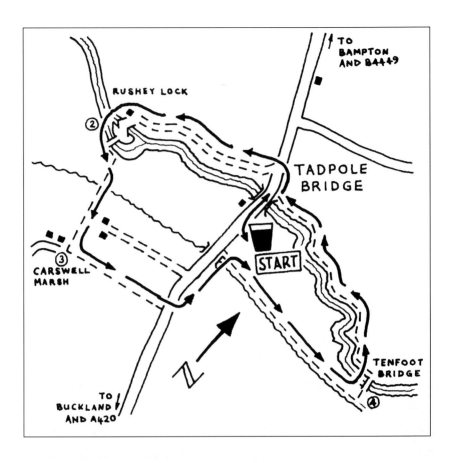

Meadow reserve. Beyond this the river continues to meander with plantations on the far bank and old willows on this side; again nettles can be a problem. Eventually the path emerges into open pastureland. Negotiate a stile and pass under a line of pylons. As you approach Tadpole Bridge you go into a scrubby stretch of land, with boats moored on the far bank. When you reach the bridge, turn left and cross the river to return to the Trout.

PLACES OF INTEREST NEARBY
Buckland Warren is an attractive area of mixed woodland to the south of the A420 at Buckland. Nearby are two dovecotes, both Grade II listed – one at Home Farm near Buckland, the other near Pusey. Buckland also has a splendid church, which well repays a visit.

CULHAM, SUTTON COURTENAY AND SUTTON POOLS

This walk starts by the village stocks on Culham village green, then leads via a series of weirs to Sutton Courtenay. The churchyard at Sutton contains the graves of Herbert Asquith and George Orwell, and the village has some historic buildings as well as a network of intriguing paths through which this route winds. As well as two sections along the River Thames, part of this walk follows pretty Ginge Brook as it rushes towards its confluence with the larger river.

Sutton Bridge

Culham is a quiet village on a side road off the A415. Its handsome manor house, glimpsed early in this walk, includes a 15th-century wing that was probably part of a grange of the abbots of Abingdon. The pretty church sits at the end of an attractive village green which sports a set of stocks. The old village once extended further towards the river, but there is nothing to be seen but humps and bumps in the fields now.

71

The cause of its decline is a matter for conjecture.

Sutton Courtenay is a larger village with a fascinating history. 'Sutton' refers to its position as the 'south farm' of Abingdon; Courtenay is in central France, near the famous Chablis wine region, from whence came Reginald de Courtenay, who was given the manor by Henry II in the 12th century. The oldest visible artefact in the village is probably not the Norman church tower, or the late Norman hall opposite (a survival of a royal 'vill'), but rather the causeway that divides the millstream from the weirstream at Sutton Pools. This is reckoned to have been originally constructed in Saxon times (probably in the late 10th century), and would have required huge amounts of manpower and no little engineering prowess.

Alongside the millstream is a picturesque half-timbered building right on the water's edge. This is known as the Wharf Barn, and old photographs show it with barges tied up in front and cargoes piled all around. The barn stands in the grounds of a house known as The Wharf, which was home to H. H. Asquith, the last Liberal prime minister, and his wife Margot. She had the barn converted for her personal use, with a sitting room downstairs and a bedroom upstairs. The neighbouring Mill House was given by Lord and Lady Wantage (see Walk 18) to a cousin of theirs, Captain Harry Lindsay, and was a popular weekend destination for members of the social circle of the then Prince of Wales.

The mill itself, now demolished except for the brick wall flanking the bridge by which you cross the millstream, was a paper mill (as was Sandford Mill on Walk 12). From 1697 until 1724 the miller had the contract for making special banknote paper for the Bank of England (which had only been founded in 1694 and suffered greatly at the hands of forgers).

The Lion at Culham is an unpretentious local pub serving Morrells beers and a range of reasonably priced, traditionally prepared food, available at lunchtime and in the evening. The menu includes sandwiches, bar snacks, vegetarian options and roasts on Sundays, with children's portions to order. Occasional barbecues take place in the garden in summer. You are advised to book to avoid delays, especially at weekends. Children and dogs are welcome. Pub games include Aunt Sally, darts and pool. Telephone: 01235 520327.

This route also passes all of Sutton Courtenay's four remaining pubs: the George and Dragon and the Swan on the green, the Plough in the High Street and the Fish at the end of All Saints Lane. All are worth a visit; the last-mentioned is renowned for its gourmet cuisine, served in an attractive conservatory.

- **HOW TO GET THERE:** Culham can be reached from the A415 just east of Abingdon. Having left the town via Abingdon Bridge and driven along the ancient Causeway, take the first right, signposted to Culham. The Lion is on the outside of a bend, by the green at the beginning of the village.
- **PARKING:** Patrons may leave their cars in the pub car park (with permission) while they walk; there is street parking nearby.
- **LENGTH OF THE WALK:** 3¾ miles. Maps: OS Landranger 164 Oxford, Chipping Norton and Bicester or 174 Newbury and Wantage, Hungerford and Didcot; OS Explorer 170 Abingdon, Wantage and Vale of White Horse (GR 503950).

THE WALK

1. Follow the footpath that leads away from the main village street to the left of the Lion, to a pair of gates beside a converted barn. Keep along the field edge to the Culham Cut, which you cross via the footbridge (look right for a glimpse of Culham Manor and the church). Beyond the bridge a path leads away from the river, crossing a bridge and passing a Second World War pillbox. Cross the weir bridge and follow the footpath along the old causeway, crossing three smaller weirs. At the site of the old mill the path swings right, crosses the millstream on a footbridge and joins Church Street in Sutton Courtenay.

2. Turn right and walk along between two rows of attractive houses, then pass Norman Hall on the right, the George and Dragon pub on the left and the church, also on the left, in quick succession. Beyond the village green a little further along is the Swan pub. Keep along the main road, passing the entrance to Sutton Manor, to a triangular junction, where you keep right towards Drayton and Steventon, passing the entrance to Chapel Lane on the opposite side of the road. Cross Ginge Brook then walk along a driveway on the left that follows the stream. At the end of the driveway, a row of houses straddles the stream; go through the gate to the right, into a field. Keep along the left-hand edge of this field, to a double-stile with a footbridge, which leads into an attractive field with ridge and furrow and the stream running through it. Keep along the stream to a track where you cross a stile and turn left. The stream follows the road then passes under it by Upper Mill; keep straight on up the lane to emerge on the High Street by the Plough pub.

3. Turn right for a short distance, then take a narrow walled path on the left by the postbox. When this path emerges into open fields, turn

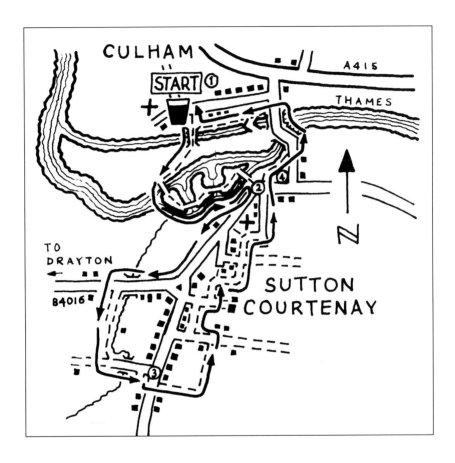

left, and keep to the left along a belt of scrubby trees. Beyond this follow a fenced path to emerge in a lane by some houses. Turn left and then take the first available track on the right. Pass a tennis court on the right and an old barn on the left. When you reach a T-junction of tracks, turn right and then swing left at the entrance to a farm. This track swings right and then left, and then crosses another track into All Saints Lane. When the lane swings right to skirt the church, you can either enter the graveyard via a metal gate and cut across diagonally right to another gate (and seek out the graves of Asquith, and Orwell – marked with his real name, Eric Blair – on the way), or you can follow the track. Whichever you choose, when you reach a concrete road, turn left. The track passes the car park of the Fish and re-emerges on the B4016. Cross straight over into a driveway opposite.

Sutton Pools

4. At the end of the driveway a stile leads into a meadow, with the sound of a small weir audible in the gardens of Mill House on your left. Keep along the left-hand edge of the field until you reach the river, where there are beautiful views of Sutton Bridge (built 1807) downstream. Walk right along the riverbank until a gate leads up to the road some distance short of the bridge. Cross over and turn left past the traffic lights. Cross both bridges, then turn left through a gate onto the towpath. Walk past Culham Lock (one of the two deepest on the Thames; the other is at Sandford – see Walk 12). Beyond the lock compound, keep along the Cut until you reach the footbridge you crossed earlier. Here turn right and retrace your steps to Culham.

PLACES OF INTEREST NEARBY

Abingdon Museum is housed in the 17th-century County Hall in Abingdon's Market Square. Admission is free. The galleries contain artefacts ranging from neolithic stone implements to 20th-century memorabilia from the MG Motor Works (which closed in the late 1970s). Telephone: 01235 723703 or follow links from http://www.oxfordshire.gov.uk/

DORCHESTER-ON-THAMES: TWO RIVERS AND A LOCK

Dorchester, with its magnificent Abbey and the ancient earthworks of the Dyke Hills as reminders of its former importance, is located near the confluence of the Thame and the Thames. This short, easy walk samples both, as well as giving a flavour of the ancient village. It may be extended across the footbridge at Day's Lock to visit pretty Little Wittenham, or the energetic may choose to tackle the stiff climb to Wittenham Clumps and back.

The River Thame, near Dorchester

Look at the index of any book on the history of Oxfordshire, and you will find many references to Dorchester-on-Thames, for historically this is one of the county's earliest and most important settlements. There is evidence of an Iron Age 'oppidum' (a fortified urban settlement) here, around the time the large earthworks of the Dyke Hills were constructed. The Romans built a walled town in the locality, hence the

Roman *cester* suffix. After a period of decline in the Dark Ages, Birinus, an Italian missionary, chose Dorchester as the capital of his see and founded the Abbey there in the 7th century. The relics of St Birinus were transported back to Dorchester from Winchester in the 13th century and the town became a place of pilgrimage.

Nowadays the Dyke Hills are much reduced and Dorchester is a peaceful and pretty settlement of old houses clustered around the great abbey building.

The Plough at Dorchester is not the village's best-known pub, but it is a personal favourite of mine. The cosy and friendly interior boasts a well-thumbed library, an open fireplace, and many interesting pictures. The food is genuinely homemade and consists of delicious and inventive casseroles and stews, always including at least one vegetarian option, served in earthenware bowls with granary bread and a hunk of real butter. The wine selection is also a cut above average and beers come from the Morrells brewery. Food is served at lunchtime and in the evening, except Tuesday evenings. Children and dogs are welcome in the garden only. Telephone: 01865 340012.

- **HOW TO GET THERE:** Dorchester-on-Thames is bypassed by the A4074. Take the A415 at the Berinsfield roundabout and then go left; the Plough is on the right at the entrance to the village.
- **PARKING:** Patrons may leave their cars in the pub car park (with permission) while they walk; there is ample street parking in Drayton Road opposite, and elsewhere nearby.
- **LENGTH OF THE WALK:** 4 miles. Maps: OS Landranger 164 Oxford, Chipping Norton and Bicester or 174 Newbury and Wantage, Hungerford and Didcot; OS Explorer 170 Abingdon, Wantage and Vale of White Horse (GR 576947).

THE WALK

1. Having read today's *bon mots* on the blackboard by the front door of the Plough, cross the High Street and walk down Drayton Road. Once past the playing field on your left, you reach Dorchester Lake (also known as Cemetery Pit), a flooded gravel pit now thoroughly naturalised. Keep straight on along the road with the lake to your left. At the foot of the bridge over the Dorchester bypass, by the last streetlight, turn right into a footpath. This leads along the back of gardens with an open field to the left. Ignore three right-hand turns until you cross the River Thame by a concrete footbridge to enter Hurst watermeadow. This open space was purchased for the village, with the assistance of a grant from the 'landfill tax', in 1996. Those in a hurry can walk straight across the meadow; the rest turn left and walk upstream along the western arm of the Thame. Follow it around to the right to an old weir. Here turn right and walk parallel to the other leg of the Thame (the millstream) until you regain the footpath you left earlier by a stile and footbridge. Turn left and cross the millstream by picturesque Overy Mill. This path shortly emerges in a side lane that soon joins the main lane in the hamlet of Overy. Turn right and walk down the lane, past handsome houses and cottages of 'clunch' (hard chalk) and brick, and with glimpses of the abbey to your right, to the main road.

2. Turn right and cross the Thame once more via Dorchester Bridge. Beyond the bridge our route turns left into Bridge End (but you may wish to take this opportunity to visit the Abbey and its adjacent museum and tearoom). Keep along Bridge End past the Catholic church of St Birinus, then keep left past the Chequers pub to a small teardrop-shaped village green. At the far end of a terrace of cottages on the right, take a narrow footpath that leads to the right through gardens to a gravelly drive by a thatched cottage. Turn left and when the drive swings right follow the path ahead along a field edge towards the banks of the Dyke Hills, with Wittenham Clumps as a dominant backdrop. At the end of the Dyke Hills, pass through a metal kissing gate and walk past a Second World War pillbox. Keep on in the same approximate direction to a further kissing gate. Beyond this gate aim for the outside of a meander in the Thame, and then keep on to the Thames by the low bridge at the confluence of the two rivers. Turn right along the Thames towpath.

3. At the end of the field pass through a wooden gate into a hedged stretch of towpath as it approaches the steep slopes of Wittenham Clumps on the far bank. Follow the river until it curves right to a footbridge at Day's Lock, with Little Wittenham beyond. Pass under the footbridge, then walk diagonally away from the river to the right (in the approximate direction of the Abbey tower), along a slight causeway to a gate. Beyond this point the path runs between fences and hedges to cross the Dyke Hills once more.

4. Swing right across a farm track and walk alongside the northern embankment, then halfway along turn left across the field towards Dorchester. At the far side the path runs between gardens to emerge in

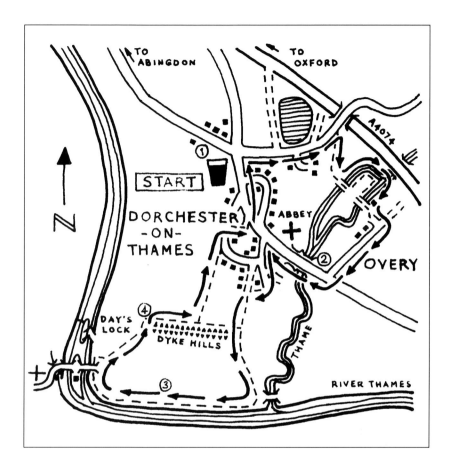

Watling Lane. Turn left by the allotments. Just past Orchard Cottage and the Old Malt House, turn right down a narrow walled path. This emerges by a pretty thatched terrace where you turn left to regain the old main road through Dorchester. Keep left to return to the Plough.

PLACES OF INTEREST NEARBY

The *Pendon Museum* at Long Wittenham (west of Dorchester via the charming village of Clifton Hampden) specialises in model railways and includes a model of the village as it appeared in the 1930s. For more information, telephone 01865 407365 or visit the website at http://dialspace.dial.pipex.com/sfb/pendon.htm.

THE THAMES AT WALLINGFORD

This walk, along both banks of the River Thames, is a route of contrasting pairs: it uses two very different road bridges over the Thames, visits two redundant churches and follows two ancient earthworks. It even follows short sections of two different long-distance footpaths, namely the Thames Path and the Ridgeway Path. It includes sections in the historic and attractive town of Wallingford, one of the oldest settlements in Britain, and some pretty Thames-side country to boot.

The Thames at Wallingford

From prehistoric times, Wallingford lay at a strategically important point, the lowest place at which the river could be forded at any time of year. (The first record of a bridge was in 1141, and some of the stonework in the existing bridge dates back to the 16th century.) Wallingford was arguably at the peak of its importance in Saxon times, when it had its own mint and was probably the largest defended town in the kingdom of Wessex. The ancient ramparts, well over 1,000 years old, still present a notable barrier in places (seen well during this walk). Wallingford Castle, which can also be visited en route, was founded in 1067, one of the earliest in England, and grew to be among the largest at one stage. Now only a few fragments remain, although the Norman mound, or motte, is still impressive; the largest surviving ruin is not actually part of the castle, but the remains of the Collegiate Church of St Nicholas. The Castle Gardens form an attractive public park.

The redundant churches of St John at Mongewell and St Mary at Newnham Murren are both worth a look (keys available). The former, a strange mixture of restored Norman and ruined 18th-century Gothic, has a peculiar setting by the river within the grounds of Carmel College, formerly one of the country's leading Jewish colleges. The latter, a simple flint building next to a farmhouse, has a Norman north doorway and chancel arch.

The Coach and Horses is a friendly and welcoming pub with a flower-hung patio overlooking the Saxon fortifications and the open space of Kinecroft. Inside you will find a traditional local with that increasingly rare feature, a piano. The pub is open all day in summer, and normal winter hours. On Sunday lunchtimes traditional roast dinners are available. Beers are from the well-regarded Fuller's Brewery in Chiswick. Dogs are allowed in the back bar and on the patio; well-behaved children are welcome. Telephone: 01491 825054.

- **HOW TO GET THERE:** Wallingford can be reached from the A4074 to the north via Shillingford Bridge, from the east via Wallingford Bridge, from the south on the A329, and from the west on the A4130. From the A4130 Didcot road just west of the light-controlled crossroads in the centre of Wallingford, turn south into Goldsmith's Lane. The Coach and Horses is in Kinecroft, a turning on the right-hand side about 100 yards from the main road.

- **PARKING:** There is limited free parking next to the pub, or a large (and reasonably cheap) pay-and-display car park near the junction of Kinecroft and Goldsmith's Lane. On summer evenings, you may be able to benefit from the fact that the car park is free after 6 pm.

- **LENGTH OF THE WALK:** 4½ miles or 3 miles if you omit the Mongewell loop. Maps: OS Landranger 175 Reading and Windsor; OS Explorer 170 Abingdon, Wantage and Vale of White Horse (GR 605893).

THE WALK

1. From the Coach and Horses, set off along the tarmac path that crosses the green of Kinecroft diagonally left towards the corner of the Saxon earthwork. On reaching the bank, climb the steps and turn left to follow a path along the top of the embankment. This emerges into a lane by the quaintly named Beansheaf Terrace and continues via Mill Lane to the main road. Turn right until you reach the end of St John's Road, from which point you can escape the traffic by following Squires Walk to the right of St John's Green. This leads behind the houses and alongside the boundary of Wallingford Hospital until it returns you to the main road. Just beyond the hospital entrance cross the main road and follow a pretty path that leads alongside Bradford Brook to the River Thames. Turn right and follow the towpath downstream.

2. The towpath leads through a series of gates as it approaches Winterbrook Bridge (opened in 1993 to carry the new Wallingford bypass). Do not pass under the bridge, but just before you reach it, head right to a gate. Notice the huge concrete flood arches to the right of the main span. These may look very different, but fulfil the same purpose as the subsidiary arches in the old Wallingford Bridge: to prevent the backup of water and to reduce the flow through the main span in times of flood. Walk up the zigzag ramp to the roadside and turn left to cross the river.

3. After a noisy hundred yards or so, you reach a bridleway, which passes under the Wallingford bypass through its own underpass. You can shorten your walk by 1½ miles by turning left here and skipping to point 5. Otherwise, walk under the road and follow the Ridgeway Path straight ahead on the other side. This leads shortly to the road at Mongewell and the first buildings of Carmel College. Look out on the right for the signposted footpath to St John's church; this leads incongruously through modern buildings and to the right of a landscaped inlet of the Thames, past an impressive weeping beech tree (with its own encircling ditch) to the church. Return via the same route.

4. Keep on along the road, passing the end of Mongewell Lake on the left. Beyond the lake is a driveway, then our route swings left into Judge's Ride. Follow this quiet road for nearly ½ mile until you reach the A4074. Turn left and walk along the verge, past the entrance to Carmel. Just beyond it, take a bridleway on the left (signposted with a Ridgeway

Path sign). Ignore the footpath that heads off to the right, instead follow the low ridge of Grim's Ditch on the left as it descends gently through a belt of woodland. This attractive path edges gradually closer and closer to the A4130 Wallingford bypass until it reaches the roadside at a kissing gate. Turn left and walk along the road to reach the underpass again, and return to the other side of the road.

5. Walk northwards, away from the bypass, past industrial buildings to the right along an otherwise attractive hedged path. You soon reach the flint building of St Mary's church, Newnham Murren. Pass the church and the adjoining farmhouse, then head over a stile between farm buildings and a couple of modern houses. This path leads past the farm and then through a kissing gate into a meadow. Head left to the

83

river's edge and follow it upstream. Cross a ditch more or less opposite St Leonard's church on the far bank and continue past elegant riverside dwellings and the headquarters of Wallingford Rowing Club. Cross another sidestream via a footbridge, then walk under the arch of Wallingford Bridge nearest the river. Turn back on yourself and climb the stone stairs to the pavement. Turn right and walk across the bridge into Wallingford.

6. Just beyond the Mill House pub and restaurant on the right is Castle Lane. A right of way from the end of this lane cuts through the Castle Gardens and provides a more interesting route to the beginning of the next paragraph than that described here; however, at the time of writing it is temporarily closed because of a dangerously unstable wall. If the diversion signs are still in evidence when you visit, continue along the High Street, passing the 15th-century George Hotel. At the traffic lights turn right into Castle Street. Pass a small car park and the entrance to the Castle Gardens on the right. Shortly beyond this is the far end of the Castle Lane footpath.

7. Keep on along the road until you reach open country, with the moat and outer earthworks of the castle obvious on the right. Just beyond The Old Schoolhouse, take a narrow shady path on the left. This leads past a building, then opens out with tennis courts on the right and the impressive ditch and bank of the Saxon ramparts on the left. Just before you reach a road, turn left and walk down and up across the ramparts to enter a park. Follow the path to the right, then branch diagonally left across the park towards a children's play area. Beyond this, follow the path to the park entrance. Here turn right, and pass the entrance to Goldsmith's Lane on the other side of the road. Opposite Wallingford Museum, housed in the medieval Flint House, cross the road and walk across Kinecroft back to the Coach and Horses.

PLACES OF INTEREST NEARBY

The *Cholsey and Wallingford Railway* runs diesel and visiting steam trains along the old 'Wallingford bunk', the branch line from the main GWR line at Cholsey. The Wallingford terminus is in St John's Road on the southern edge of the town. There is a gift shop, a café and a museum exhibiting a model of the original station with an N-gauge railway. Limited opening; for more information telephone 01491 835067 or see http://homepages.uel.ac.uk/1278/rly-pres/cwr.html.

ARDINGTON, LOCKINGE AND GINGE: A STREAMSIDE STROLL

This is a delightful walk through pretty villages and along chalk streams in the shadow of the Downs. The bold hand of Lord Wantage, a pioneering Victorian landowner, is seen in the quaint estate cottages and the landscaping of the Lockinge valley. The walk begins in pretty Ardington and leads by way of Lockinge and its streamside church to Ginge. The return is via the deep cleft of Ginge Brook and another attractively located church at West Hendred.

Ardington House

In 1873 the Lockinge estate, in the ownership of Col Robert Loyd-Lindsay and incorporating the villages of Ardington, Lockinge and Ginge, was recorded as the largest in Berkshire. Loyd-Lindsay, later Lord Wantage, was awarded the VC for gallantry at the battles of Alma and Inkerman during the Crimean War.

Lord Wantage took a personal and enthusiastic interest in the workings of the estate. As tenants died or resigned their leases, he incorporated their lands into the 'home farm', run directly by the estate. He rebuilt the villages of Ardington and Lockinge, endowing them with schools and co-operative shops. Lord Wantage also commissioned the famous statue of King Alfred that stands in the centre of Wantage. An innovative agriculturalist, he instituted a profit-sharing scheme for his workers and even had postboxes erected in the fields, in which farm operatives were expected to place notes on cropping operations and yields.

Lord Wantage died in 1901 and is buried in Ardington churchyard and commemorated by a memorial on the Ridgeway above Betterton. His seat, Lockinge House, a large part-Georgian mansion close by the church, was demolished in 1947.

In contrast to Ardington and Lockinge, the hamlets of East and West Ginge and the village of West Hendred are traditional downland villages with brick and thatch much in evidence. Ginge Brook has carved itself a deep valley as it runs north from Ginge to West Hendred, and in places runs between chalk cliffs overhung by wild box bushes. The other stream encountered adopts the names of the settlements as it flows through them, so it is known as Betterton Brook, Lockinge Brook and Ardington Brook before its confluence with Ginge Brook. The resulting stream is marked as East Hendred Brook on the Ordnance Survey map, but oddly reappears as Ginge Brook shortly before its confluence with the Thames in Steventon and Sutton Courtenay, several miles downstream (see Walk 15).

Lord Wantage disapproved of drinking, and converted one of Ardington's pubs into cottages. At another, the Bull, he installed an old soldier as manager, and paid him a fixed salary with commission on sales of coffee, tea and soup only, so there was little incentive to boost alcohol sales. The Boar's Head is now the only pub in Ardington. Its à la carte menu, described by the landlord as 'combining the best of old and new French and English cuisine' is a major draw. For less formal appetites, light meals and ciabattas are also available in the bar. Three real ales are available on draught, plus seven wines by the glass. Dogs and children are welcome. The pub opens for the standard hours, except on Sunday evenings when it remains closed. Large groups are requested to book in advance. Telephone: 01235 833254.

- **HOW TO GET THERE:** Ardington is signposted from the A417 between Didcot and Wantage. In the village turn left into Church Street. The Boar's Head is next to the church.

- **PARKING:** There is limited parking (patrons only) in front of the pub – please ask permission to leave your car while you walk – and street parking nearby.
- **LENGTH OF THE WALK:** 5 miles. Maps: OS Landranger 174 Newbury and Wantage, Hungerford and Didcot; OS Explorer 170 Abingdon, Wantage and Vale of White Horse (GR 432883).

THE WALK

1. From the Boar's Head, turn left past the church. At a triangular junction, turn left. Just after the last cottage on the right, turn right along a permitted path (if the path is unavailable, keep along the road, cross the stream and follow a public footpath immediately on the right). The permitted path leads by a pond and crosses a stream by Ardington Mill, and then leads through a wooden gate into a field with the stream on the right. At the end of the field pass through another gate and turn right. Cross the stream on a rustic stone bridge at the foot of a lake and regain the road at a gate. Turn left.

2. Follow the road through Lockinge village, keeping left at the war memorial. Do not neglect to walk down the drive to Lockinge church. This lovely spot, with its naturalistic rockery and fast-flowing stream, has a northern feel and seems out of place in pastoral Oxfordshire. When you regain the road, turn left and shortly cross the stream, following the road around to the right. You pass the gates of Betterton House, then pass a turning on the left signposted to Ardington and another on the right to Betterton. The road then leads eastwards to Ginge with distant views to Oxford and rather nearer views of the Downs escarpment. Ignore a no through road at the beginning of Ginge, following the road downhill through the hamlet to the stream (often dried up at this point). Just beyond the stream, opposite an old brick-built cottage, turn left (signposted to West Hendred).

3. Our path leads along a shady way with the stream valley on the left to a stile. Beyond the stile the path gradually descends through box bushes to the stream. At one point a path joins from the left. When a second path crosses at right angles, with the smooth curve of Goldbury Hill prominent behind some houses ahead of you, turn right and walk up to the road.

4. Turn left and walk down the road into West Hendred. Turn left at the old school and into the churchyard. Cross the stream, where the

87

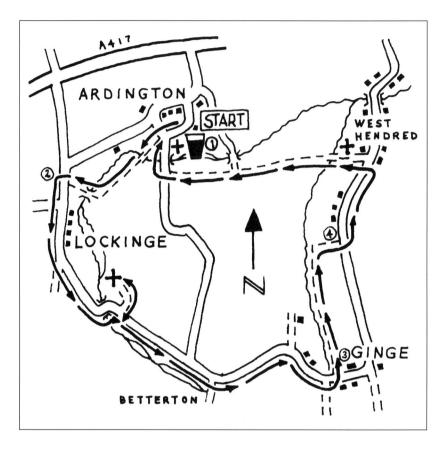

path swings left then right to lead across open fields. Beyond the buildings of Red Barn, keep straight on where a path crosses. There follows a fitting climax along Ardington Brook with fine views of the frontage of Ardington House and the church. At the road, turn right across the stream and retrace your steps to your starting point.

PLACES OF INTEREST NEARBY

The *Vale and Downland Museum and Visitor Centre* is housed in a 17th-century cloth merchant's house in Church Street, Wantage. Its galleries explore the geology, natural history, archaeology and social history of the Vale of the White Horse, and special events, such as exhibitions of local artists' work, are often held. There is a café with an attractive terrace and garden. Telephone: 01235 771447 or see http://www.wantage.com/museum/

ALONG THE THAMES BETWEEN SOUTH AND NORTH STOKE

This Thames-side walk includes two pretty villages with flint churches, two lost ferries and a marvel of Victorian engineering. The walk leads through fields from South Stoke to North Stoke and returns along the Thames, passing ferry sites at Littlestoke and the quaintly named Beetle and Wedge, and between them Brunel's brick railway viaduct carrying the Great Western Railway over the river. Parts of the walk may be muddy in wet weather.

Brunel's Moulsford Railway Bridge

By this stage in its journey through the county, the River Thames has gained the stature of a major river. There was no way of fording a river of this size, or of easily bridging it, so from here on downstream there were many ferries. With less demand from river traffic and the advent of the car, the ferries became uneconomical and were abandoned. This walk follows the disconnected piece of towpath on the eastern bank between the two ferries at Littlestoke and Beetle and Wedge. This stretch is part of the Ridgeway Path, so there are long-distance footpaths on both sides of the river at the two ferries.

South Stoke and North Stoke are built in the local materials of brick, flint and thatch. The churches are especially fine, particularly that at North Stoke, which has a Norman sundial above the blocked south doorway and splendid medieval wall paintings inside.

The Perch and Pike at South Stoke is a rose-hung 18th-century building of brick and flint on the main street near the church. It prides itself on its food, which includes open club sandwiches and steak and onion baguettes at lunchtime, both popular with walkers. There are more formal starters and main dishes on the excellent restaurant menu, including several vegetarian options, and small portions for children are available on request. Drinks include Brakspear's beers and a range of wines by the glass. You are advised to book if you wish to eat in the restaurant, especially in the evenings and at weekends. Note that the pub is closed on Sunday evenings, and dogs are welcome only at the terrace tables outside. Telephone: 01491 872415.

- **HOW TO GET THERE:** South Stoke is just off the B4009 between Goring and Wallingford. The village is E-shaped – take any of the turnings signposted off the main road and you will find the pub on the spine of the 'E', near the church.
- **PARKING:** There is ample parking at the pub for patrons (but please ask before leaving your car while you walk).There is also adequate street parking nearby.
- **LENGTH OF THE WALK:** 4¾ miles (3¼ miles if you turn back at Littlestoke). Maps: OS Landranger 175 Reading and Windsor and 174 Newbury and Wantage, Hungerford and Didcot; OS Explorer 170 Abingdon, Wantage and Vale of White Horse (GR 599835).

THE WALK

1. From the road outside the Perch and Pike, walk right, shortly passing the school and church. When the road bends right follow it towards the railway bridge. Soon afterwards, opposite a fine group of farm buildings (including a large barn, a granary and a 17th-century dovecote, the largest in Oxfordshire), follow the footpath sign down a drive on the left. Beyond the last house the path narrows and emerges into a field bounded by the railway embankment away on the right. Walk along the left-hand edge of the field, and then follow the obvious

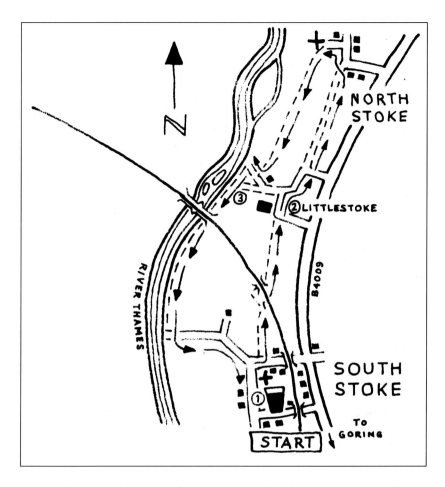

path when it leads away from the wood and curves in a wide arc towards the railway. A short stretch alongside the embankment leads to a brick tunnel by which you make your way to the eastern side. On emerging turn left, then swing right away from the railway along a weedy field boundary. The path heads off left into the next field and across it to a wooden footbridge and a high stile. Beyond this follow the fence to the right of Littlestoke Manor. This brings you out, via a stile constructed from a slab of granite inserted into the wall, into the road at Littlestoke.

2. Walk along the road with the flint walls of the Manor on your left. Keep to the road at the entrance to Little Stoke House (unless you wish

91

to shorten your route by omitting the loop to North Stoke) and follow it as it doglegs right and left. When the road finally turns right to return to the main road, follow the right of way that continues straight ahead. This leads uneventfully to North Stoke. Walk up The Street as far as Church Lane, where you turn left. (You may choose to continue for a short there-and-back diversion along the main street to the mill, where you can peer into the wheel chamber.) Church Lane leads past some pretty cottages to the lychgate. Depart the churchyard by a kissing gate behind the tower. Beyond the gate and a paddock the fenced path leads across a series of gardens with more kissing gates. Shortly the path enters open fields; keep to the right-hand edges through yet more kissing gates. When you cross a side stream and breast a slight bank you get your first proper sight of the river below. At the rear of Little Stoke House the path enters another fenced stretch through gardens, until finally reaching the river properly at Littlestoke Ferry. Here turn left along the towpath.

3. Pass a Second World War pillbox and go through a gate into open Thames meadows. Continue along the towpath, passing a group of islands to reach the railway viaduct, which was built in 1838–40 and extended in 1893. The path here can be rather muddy where cattle share the path under the railway. Beyond the bridge the towpath continues in similar vein, passing Moulsford Preparatory School and Moulsford church on the opposite bank. When you reach a lane at the site of the Beetle and Wedge ferry, turn left away from the river. (The 'beetle and wedge' were tools used to split wood, and are depicted on the sign of the renowned hotel and restaurant on the Moulsford side, sadly denied us on this walk by the lack of a crossing.) The lane leads back to South Stoke. Keep right at the entrance to Lower Farm, then turn right at the splendid Corner House (a Georgian house with an older half-timbered wing) to return to the Perch and Pike.

PLACES OF INTEREST NEARBY

Lardon Chase (NT), on the Berkshire side of the river above Streatley-on-Thames, is a downland ridge renowned for its rare butterflies and flowers, including orchids, and offers superb views over the 'Goring Gap', where the Thames cuts through the Chilterns. To reach Streatley from South Stoke, turn right on the B4009, then right again in Goring to cross the river, and continue along the B4009 in the direction of Aldworth. There is a car park on the right ½ mile out of Streatley.

THE WOODED THAMES NEAR WHITCHURCH

This contrasting walk starts in the picture-postcard village of Whitchurch-on-Thames. It continues via an interesting wooded stretch of the river and returns along some glorious Chiltern paths through typical beechwood scenery with wide views over the Goring Gap. This is a good choice of walk at times of high water, as the riverside section (along the steep bank of Hartslock Wood) is unlikely to be affected by flooding.

Whitchurch-on-Thames

Whitchurch-on-Thames is a quiet Oxfordshire village, in contrast to Pangbourne, its busy Berkshire neighbour on the opposite bank of the Thames. Part of the reason for this contrast must be the existence of the tollbridge that separates them (one of only two remaining on the Thames; the other is near Eynsham and is visited on Walk 9). The tollhouse is on the Whitchurch side, so paradoxically Pangbourne residents could enjoy the much-photographed views from the bridge of Whitchurch steeple reflected in the mill pool for free, while the parishioners would strictly have had to pay for the privilege.

Away from Whitchurch the route follows a path that has been claimed as an ancient British trackway to Hartslock Wood, the steep wooded bank of the Thames as it cuts through the chalk. The grassland above the wood is maintained as a nature reserve by the local Wildlife Trust BBOWT, and boasts downland butterflies and plants (including the rare bastard toadflax). The views to Brunel's viaduct carrying the Great Western Railway over the river (known locally as Four Arches Bridge, but more officially as Gatehampton Bridge) are spectacular.

The Greyhound Inn is a pretty late 16th-century pub on the High Street in Whitchurch. The beamed interior is welcoming and there is a refreshing absence of piped music, games machines and jukebox. A good range of freshly prepared food is served, including sandwiches and light meals, except on Sunday evenings. A selection of four real ales (including Marston's Pedigree and Flowers) is available. Dogs are welcome on leads, but children are not allowed inside the bar (there is a secluded garden to the rear that may be an option in the summer). Telephone: 0118 984 2160.

- **HOW TO GET THERE:** Whitchurch can be reached via the B471 from Woodcote to the north, or via the tollbridge from the A329 on the Berkshire bank of the river at Pangbourne. The Greyhound is on the main street 100 yards or so from the bridge.
- **PARKING:** There is a small car park in front of the Greyhound for patrons only, and limited street parking opposite and nearby.
- **LENGTH OF THE WALK:** 5¾ miles. Maps: OS Landranger 175 Reading and Windsor; OS Explorer 159 Reading, Wokingham and Pangbourne. (GR 635772).

THE WALK

1. The walk begins with a short loop to the river and back. Walk down the road towards the river and past the tollhouse onto the bridge; from the bridge look back to view the much-photographed scene of riverside cottages, mill and church. Return to the tollhouse and turn left down a driveway. In front of the mill take a narrow footpath on the right signposted to the church. The church is largely Victorian though it retains its Norman south doorway and 15th-century porch. Leave the

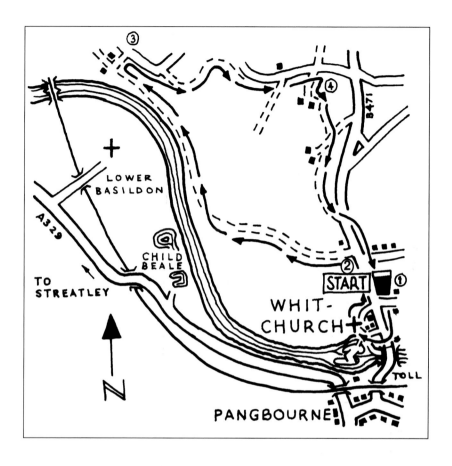

churchyard by the lychgate and follow the drive back to the main village street. Turn left and return to the Greyhound.

2. Keep on past the pub up the main street, keeping left at the junction with Hardwick Road, then turn left along a bridleway signed as the Thames Path to Goring. Follow the bridleway for about a mile, passing Long Acre Farm. At Hartslock Farm the drive ends and the path continues down some steps into a dry valley, then climbs the far side, with views to Basildon House on the far bank of the Thames floodplain. After you enter Hartslock Wood, the path descends gradually towards the river, then runs just above it for a picturesque ½ mile. As you approach the squat brick tower of Lower Basildon church (on the far bank of the river) the path leaves the wood and then the river and heads towards the hamlet of Gatehampton (with glimpses to Brunel's viaduct over the Thames). When you reach the concrete track to Gatehampton, turn right past Gattendon Lodge up a flinty track to a metalled lane.

3. Turn right along the lane, passing Gatehampton House on the right. When the road bends left, keep straight on along a track. This track shortly swings left up a valley near the entrance to the Hartslock reserve. The path snakes up the bottom of the valley and towards the top there is a spectacular view from a field gate back to the Goring Gap with the railway viaduct as the centrepiece. Eventually the path reaches the top of the hill and bends right to join a road, where you keep right. There are further views over the Thames valley. Keep on past a pair of cottages; beyond them, when a track crosses at right angles, turn right into the entrance of Coombe End Farm.

4. Just before the main group of farm buildings, the path heads left over a stile and skirts the farm to a further stile in a holly hedge. Then head left to a stile partway along a fence; beyond this the path heads straight across the middle of a field to a wood. Beyond the stile at the entrance to the wood follow the obvious path straight on through a grove of holly; a path joins from the left, but keep straight on, following the suspicion of an ancient wood bank. At a gate you leave the wood, and follow the fence ahead of you to a further gate by Beech Farm. Cross the drive and follow the path around the farm and garden to a kissing gate. A short hedged stretch follows, beyond which the path skirts a field to a further kissing gate. Our route then heads along the woodland edge of Stoneycroft Plantation, until a third gate leads down to the road. At the war memorial, cross carefully and follow the high-level path on the opposite side of the road. Walk quickly but carefully through the narrow stretch of road where there is no footpath, then follow the main street back through Whitchurch to your car.

PLACES OF INTEREST NEARBY
Beale Park at Lower Basildon is home to a collection of rare birds including owls, cranes and parrots, and child-friendly attractions include a living willow 'Mole's Maze', an adventure playground and seasonal funfair rides. Telephone: 0118 984 5172 or see http://www.henley-on-thames.org.uk/out/beale.htm.